THE OUTWARD BOUND
CANOEING HANDBOOK

THE OUTWARD BOUND®

CANOEING

HANDBOOK

PAUL LANDRY AND MATTY MCNAIR

LYONS & BURFORD,
PUBLISHERS

Printed in the United States of America

10 9 8 7 6 5 4 3 2 1

Library of Congress Cataloging-in-Publication Data

Landry, Paul A., 1954–
    The Outward Bound canoeing handbook / Paul Landry and Matty McNair.

        p. cm.
    Includes bibliographical references and index.
    ISBN 1-55821-149-7

    1. Canoes and canoeing—Handbooks, manuals, etc. 2. Canoes and canoeing—Safety measures—Handbooks, manuals, etc.
    I. McNair, Matty L.   II. Title.
    GV783.L36 1992
    797.1'22—dc20   92-11647
                                                       CIP

CONTENTS

ABOUT OUTWARD BOUND®

Outward Bound® is the oldest and largest adventure-based education program, celebrating more than fifty years of educational excellence worldwide.

Outward Bound provides experiences that enhance self-esteem and leadership skills, while buidling teamwork, positive values, compassion for others, perseverance, good citizenship and respect for the environment. Outward Bound uses the wilderness or urban environment as its 'classrooms,' and adventure and service activities as the vehicles for learning these essential life skills.

Included among more than 650 programs offered each year in the U.S. are experiences ranging in diversity from sailing, canoeing, backpacking, sea kayaking, and white-water rafting—to mountain climbing, skiing and dog sledding. Courses are conducted in 22 states, in some of the most beautiful wilderness areas in North America. To-day, Outward Bound conducts programs in urban environments in eight major U.S. cities as well.

A Brief History

Outward Bound was founded in 1941. During World War II, British merchant ships were under repeated attack from German U-boats. Surprisingly, the survival rate for those awaiting rescue in lifeboats was lowest among the younger, presumably more fit, seamen. Renowned German-born educator, Kurt Hahn, developed a program for young British seamen, whom he believed lacked the fortitude, self-reliance and perseverance that the older sailors had acquired through life experience. Hahn's program involved challenging physical and mental activities which helped build confidence, encourage compassion and instill tenacity and perseverance.

For its name, the school adopted the nautical term used when the great ships left the safety of the harbor for the open sea. They were said to be "outward bound"—bound for unknown challenges and adventures.

From this beginning, a number of Outward Bound schools were established in the United Kingdom. The movement spread to Europe and Africa; Singapore, Hong Kong, Australia and New Zealand; Canada and the United States. Today there are thirty-eight Outward Bound schools and centers in nineteen coutries on five continents.

The first U.S. Outward Bound school was established in Colorado in 1961. Today there are five Outward Bound wilderness schools in the United States: Colorado; Hurricane Island (Maine); North Carolina; Pacific Crest (Oregon); and Voyageur (Minnesota). The national headquarters for Outward Bound USA is located in Connecticut.

Outward Bound USA also has eight urban centers in the U.S., which were established as part of Outward Bound's ongoing commitment to provide its unique educational opportunities for disadvantaged urban youth. Centers are now in Atlanta, Baltimore, Boston, Denver, Los Angeles, Minneapolis/St. Paul, New York and San Francisco.

Who Outward Bound Serves

Although Outward Bound originated as a program for young men, it now offers courses for people of all ages and backgrounds. About 40% of the participants are women.

The vast majority of Outward Bound courses are open to individuals seeking to learn more about themselves. They may be students, parents, grandparents, teachers, business people—people from all walks of life, with ages ranging from 14 to 65+.

Outward Bound also offers numerous courses designed to serve the unique requirements of a variety of populations with special needs. Included are courses for adults over 50, women over 30, parents and children, couples, substance abusers, "troubled" and adjudicated youths. Programs to address the unique needs of inner-city youngsters, Vietnam veterans, alcohol and substance abusers, and specially designed courses for corporate executives, health professionals and educational groups are also offered.

Outward Bound's urban programs throughout the country have been designed to seek and act upon opportunities to help address educational and societal issues affecting the welfare of inner-city youths.

Outward Bound Courses

Today, Outward Bound courses range from 4-days to 3-months in duration. Youth courses are typically 2- to 4-weeks in length, while most adult courses are about a week long. Specific activities vary with the location and season.

Outward Bound courses involve both individual and group challenges. There is a primary focus on personal and interpersonal growth using the activities in which extensive technical training is given, such as mountaineering, canoeing, sailing, backpacking, canyoneering, whitewater rafting, dog sledding, and skiing.

During the early part of each course, students participate in activities like running, hiking and swimming—activites contributing to physical conditioning.

Participants are also provided extensive technical instruction and safety training appropriate to the activity, environment and season in which the course is conducted. Students are taught the use of specialized equipment and wilderness first aid procedures. Participants are also given instruction in the practical skills of: field food planning and preparation, map and compass use, routefinding and expedition planning. Care and protection of the environment are key elements taught in all Outward Bound courses.

After an initial training phase, participants in groups of eight to twelve take part in one or more short expeditions (mountain climbing, sailing, rafting, backpacking, canoeing, skiing) and, accompanied by an instructor, an extended journey. In longer courses, there is usually a final expedition which is student planned and led with minimal instructor supervision.

Later, with a minimum of equipment, each student has a 'solo', from a few hours to 3-days long. During this period of quiet solitude in a designated area, there are daily safety checks by an instructor. This is not a survival test! It is a time for reflection, personal goal setting and journal writing.

Rock climbing, rappelling and a ropes course are activities common to many Outward Bound courses. A group service project, journal writing, and time for the group to share thoughts and feelings about lessons learned at Outward Bound and how they can be applied back home—are integral parts of the Outward Bound experience.

Courses usually conclude with a final personal-challenge event, demonstrating to the participants that they are capable of far more than they had previously thought possible.

Safety in the Wilderness

Nearly 30,000 people each year come to Outward Bound adventure education courses in the United States. Safety is unquestionably Outward Bound's first priority. The organization's exemplary safety record reflects the importance it places on ensuring the well-being of students entrusted to its care.

No one can guarantee complete immunity from danger. However, Outward Bound's operating procedures and professional staff ensure that course activites are as safe as human ingenuity can make them, and that the risks during course activities are more perceived than real.

Lessons Learned

After an Outward Bound experience, students learn to expect more of themselves, and gain confidence where before they were hesitant. They learn to share, to lead and to follow, and to work together as a group. In safeguarding each other, they form bonds of mutual trust. They discover that cooperation among group members is essential for successful problem solving.

Traveling many miles across mountains, lakes or ocean may mean aching muscles, sore feet and tired bodies, but it also brings mutual respect, shared jokes, beautiful sunrises and the pride of shared achievement. Δ

INTRODUCTION

CANOEING can enrich your life. It can lead you to wilderness camping adventures or to the challenges of whitewater. Canoeing can also give you a peaceful and reflective time away from phones and a busy life. With a few basic skills, the joys of paddling can be yours.

After reading this book you will understand:

• how to choose proper canoeing equipment to match your needs and budget;

• the key points to efficient paddling strokes;

- the techniques of lining, tracking, or portaging your canoe around hazards;

- what to do in order to prevent serious accidents and how to respond in the event of a mishap;

- how to plan a weekend canoe trip or wilderness expedition;

- the way to safely paddle through waves and wind and what to do when caught in a thunderstorm;

- the basic skills for playing in whitewater;

- how to care for the wilderness environment through which you paddle.

The Outward Bound Canoeing Handbook is the result of our combined knowledge and experience. We have devoted many years to "canoe-based" Outward Bound Schools in North America and we are both avid wilderness canoeists. Our personal experience, expertise in teaching, and work with Outward Bound have come together in the writing of this book.

We hope that *The Outward Bound Canoeing Handbook* will help you gain the skills and knowledge needed to canoe down around the next bend in the river, portage on to the next lake, or play in the rapids.

May canoeing enrich your life.

MATTY MCNAIR AND PAUL LANDRY
Iqaluit, Northwest Territories, Canada
January 1992

1

EQUIPMENT

~~~~

USING THE APPROPRIATE CANOE equipment will definitely enhance the development of your paddling skills. But remember, appropriate does not necessarily mean expensive or of the latest design. It simply means the best match in price, quality, and design to fit your particular needs. In this chapter we will review four different canoe designs, paddles, lifevests, and canoe camping equipment such as Duluth packs, wanigans, and pack baskets. We will also offer you ideas on how to properly customize your canoe.

Canoeing equipment has changed drastically during the last decade. From the days of "all-purpose" canoes, manufacturers are now producing a variety of specialized equipment made from diverse materials with price tags that reflect a range of quality. As you read through catalogs and listen to salespeople, the variety of options can become increasingly confusing.

The first step in purchasing canoe equipment is to identify your needs. Do you want the latest racing canoe or an inexpensive boat to leave down at the pond? Do you want an aesthetically pleasing wooden paddle or one that will hold up to abuse?

The second step is to understand the differences in design characteristics (extreme rocker versus no rocker) and the strengths and weaknesses of different materials (wood, aluminum, ABS, and fiberglass).

CANOES

Before you borrow, rent, or buy a canoe, let's go over canoe terminology and design characteristics.

Terminology

WIDTH is measured at the widest point across the gunwales or at the widest point at the tumblehome (see tumblehome, below).

DEPTH is measured at the center, from the bottom of the

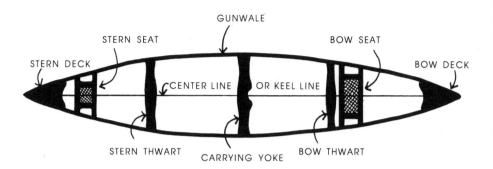

1-1. Canoe, top view.

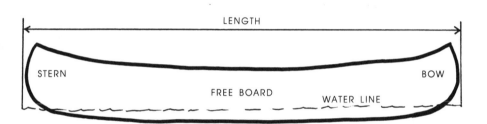

1-2. Canoe, side view.

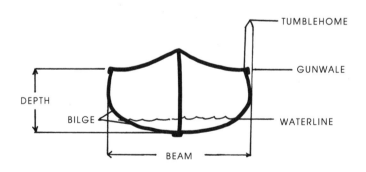

1-3. Canoe, end view.

canoe to the gunwale. A canoe with a lot of depth (high sides) will increase your carrying capacity.

CARRYING CAPACITY is the amount of weight a canoe is designed to safely carry.

FREEBOARD is measured from the water line to the top of the gunwale at the center of the canoe. Your canoe loaded for a wilderness trip should have at least six inches of freeboard.

TRIM is the balance of freeboard from bow to stern and from side to side. "Trim" your canoe by shifting packs or your position so that the bow rides slightly higher than the stern. This prevents the bow of the canoe from plowing through the water.

DRAFT is measured from the water line to the bottom of the canoe at its deepest point.

TRACK refers to how easily a canoe maintains a straight course.

ROCKER refers to the curve along the keel line, along the bottom of the canoe, from bow to stern. A canoe with little rocker is easy to keep on a straight course. A canoe with a lot of rocker will be easy to turn but will track poorly.

FLARE AND TUMBLEHOME are the terms used to describe the shape of the canoe from the water line to the gunwales. A canoe with flared sides will deflect waves and be more stable when leaned. A canoe with tumblehome loses stability quickly when leaned but is narrower and more efficient to paddle.

TANDEM PADDLING refers to two people paddling a canoe, one in the bow, the other in the stern.

SOLO PADDLING is one person paddling a canoe from the center or just behind the center.

Canoe Designs

For simplicity we have grouped canoes into four categories: the marathon canoe, designed for speed; the expedition canoe, for touring; the recreational river canoe, for wilderness whitewater; and the slalom canoe, for maneuverability. Each canoe is designed for a specific purpose.

Marathon Canoe*

Length: 18.5′	Depth: 11.5″
Width: 32″	Weight: 30–55 lbs.

These canoes are designed to travel quickly through the water. They are high-performance canoes used by experts for sprint, marathon, and downriver racing. These boats

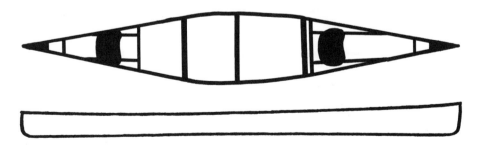

1-4. Marathon canoe

*average dimensions

are long and narrow, making them tippy for novice paddlers. Their straight keel line makes them track efficiently but turn with difficulty. These lightweight canoes are built of fiberglass or a cedar strip shell covered with fiberglass.

Expedition Canoe*

Length 17'–18'	Depth 12.5"–13.5"
Width 33"	Weight 65–85 lbs.

Expedition canoes are designed for extended wilderness trips. Compared to marathon canoes they do not track as well, are more stable, and have more depth, which increases their carrying capacity. They are designed with more rocker than the marathon canoes and therefore are easier to turn. Expedition canoes are manufactured in aluminum, cedar strip, fiberglass, ABS, and other plastics.

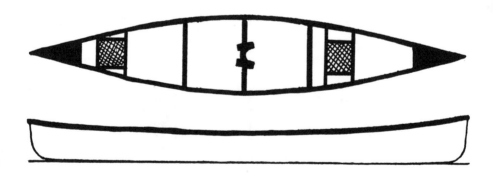

1-5. Expedition canoe

*average dimensions

Recreational River Canoe*

Length 15'–16.5'   Depth 13.5"

Width 33"–34"   Weight 65–85 lbs.

Recreational river canoes are designed for whitewater river trips and recreational whitewater. They are easier to turn than expedition canoes but do not track as well. Recreational river canoes are built of aluminum, fiberglass, and ABS plastic.

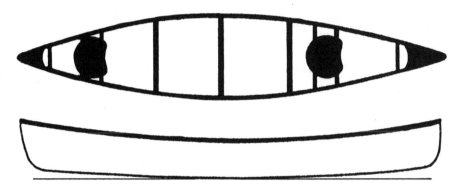

1-6. Recreational canoe

Slalom Canoe*

Length 14'–16'   Depth 12"

Width 34"   Weight 45–60 lbs.

Designed to play the rapids, slalom canoes offer excellent maneuverability. They are short and have round bottoms and a high degree of rocker. Slalom canoes com-

*average dimensions

promise durability for lightweight high performance. Paddled by experienced paddlers, they are a fun whitewater play boat. But these canoes are not enjoyable to paddle on a long expedition as it is against their nature to track straight.

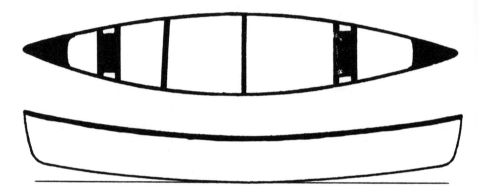

1-7. Slalom canoe

Canoe Construction

Many years ago (and still today in far-off places) boats were built of hollowed logs, bunches of reeds, or animal skins stretched over frames. One of the earliest ancestors of the canoe was the North American birch bark canoe built of split and bent wooden ribs covered with the bark of birch trees.

CEDAR STRIP CANOES are direct descendants of the birch bark canoe. A frame of wood ribs is planked over with thin cedar boards and covered with painted canvas or fiberglass. Cedar strip canoes have classic lines and are beautiful to look at, but they must be carefully maintained and paddled with respect. They are still built today both commercially and by talented individuals.

ALUMINUM CANOES were introduced after World War II. These canoes are durable, virtually maintenance-free, and can withstand abuse. However, they are cold to sit in, noisy to paddle, and difficult to repair. Aluminum canoes have a conservative design and are widely used by average summer camps and recreational paddlers.

FIBERGLASS CANOES were first introduced in the mid-1950s. Fiberglass gained popularity because molds are inexpensive to build, the design possibilities are endless, and the canoes are lightweight and easy to repair. Most competitive canoes are made of fiberglass. However, fiberglass canoes lack the abrasion and impact resistance of aluminum or ABS canoes, and over time fiberglass becomes brittle.

Fiberglass consists of fibers of glass woven into a cloth which is then saturated with a liquid resin. The strength of fiberglass canoes depends on the type and combination of materials used and the method by which they are constructed. The common cloths used are E-glass, S-glass, nylon, and Dupont's Kevlar.® Types of resin include polyester, vinylester, and epoxy. Kevlar is a stronger cloth and will produce a lighter but more expensive canoe. Before buying a fiberglass canoe, be sure to find out how it was constructed. A cheap "Kevlar" canoe may only contain twenty percent Kevlar and the rest is glass.

ABS (ACRYLONITRILE-BUTADIENE-STYRENE) was developed by Uniroyal and consists of a foam core covered by two layers of hard rubber material. Delivered to canoe manufacturers in large sheets, ABS is then molded into canoes and trimmed with wood, aluminum, or plastic to make gunwales, thwarts, and seats. ABS is tough, durable, and requires little maintenance. It will flex, slide easily over rocks, and take a tremendous bashing. The outer plastic skin wears off when dragged over rocks. ABS canoes are heavy and difficult to repair.

Customizing Your Canoe

CARRYING YOKES are worth installing if you plan to portage (carry) your canoe. A good yoke will distribute the weight of your canoe evenly on your shoulders. There are two types of yokes. One type bolts on over your existing center thwart and usually comes with foam pads for your shoulders. The other type of yoke replaces your center thwart, is made of hardwood, and is curved to fit your shoulders.

PAINTERS are the ropes attached to the ends of your canoe. They are used to tie down your canoe during transport, tie up at a dock, tow another canoe, and line or track a canoe around rapids. Painters made of three-eights-inch bright yellow polypropylene rope work best since they float and are easy to see in the water. For general recreational paddling ten- to twelve-foot painters are sufficient. On wilderness trips where lining rapids (guiding your canoe down rapids with the use of ropes) is a possibility, attach twenty- to twenty-five-foot painters.

Many canoes, particularly ABS canoes, have places to attach the painters on the bow and stern decks. This is fine for the cottage. However, if you plan to do any lining you will need to attach the painters closer to the water line. Otherwise when lining a rapid you will roll the canoe over when you pull it to shore (see chapter 3, "Lining, Tracking, and Portaging"). To install painters, drill holes just above the water line, glue in a rubber hose, and thread the painter through.

ADDITIONAL FLOTATION You may want to add more flotation to your canoe if you are paddling wilderness rivers or whitewater or if you are paddling with nonswimmers. The most inexpensive flotation is a truck inner tube pushed in under the center thwart and inflated. Commercial flotation —large plastic air bags with inflation tubes or preshaped foam blocks—can be purchased for the mid-section and ends of the canoe. Secure your flotation into the canoe to ensure it will not shift and trap you in the canoe if you capsize.

PORTAGING PADDLES Carrying paddles on a portage is awkward and leaves you without free hands to swat mosquitoes. On a Grumman canoe you can shove the blades of your paddles under the bow thwart and over the bow seat and center thwart. Overlapping the blades helps to keep them in place. On other canoes you can attach an elastic bungee cord to hold the paddle blades to the bottom of the bow seat and tie the paddle shafts to the center thwart.

PADDLES

There is a wide variety of paddle designs, construction materials, and prices. A strong, well-balanced, light paddle will be expensive but will be a dependable partner for many years. Length, blade width, and grip shape depend on the type of canoeing you plan to do, your size, your strength, and your personal preference. Before you buy your own paddle, try as many different types as possible.

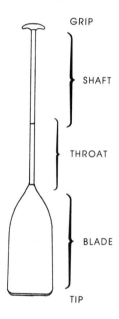

GRIP

SHAFT

THROAT

BLADE

TIP

1-8. Paddle.

There are some *general* guidelines to consider when purchasing a paddle:

1. Standard length is up to the chin; however, you may want it shorter or longer. Try different lengths.

2. The blade width generally varies from six to eight inches. Wider blades are used in whitewater, longer, narrower blades for lake travel.

3. Pear-shaped grips on lake paddles fit comfortably in the palm of your hand while T-grips offer more blade control in whitewater.

CLASSIC WOOD PADDLES are built from a single piece of hardwood, usually cherry, ash, elm, or maple. The long,

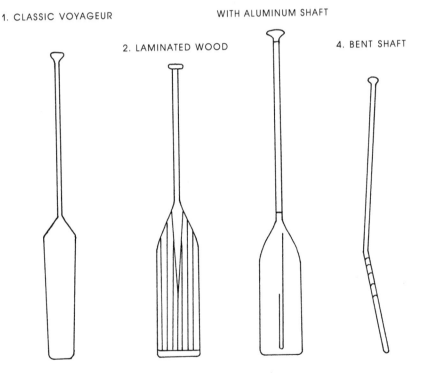

1. CLASSIC VOYAGEUR

2. LAMINATED WOOD

3. FIBERGLASS OR PLASTIC BLADE WITH ALUMINUM SHAFT

4. BENT SHAFT

1-9. Paddle types.

narrow blades, thin shafts, and pear-shaped handles are aesthetically pleasing. These paddles have a lively spring action and lend themselves well to paddling with a quick tempo in deep water. They do require maintenance to prevent them from warping and cracking.

LAMINATED WOOD PADDLES combine softwood for lightness with hardwood inserted in the shafts, blades, and tips for strength. Good laminated paddles are expensive and need a yearly coat of marine varnish but are a joy to use.

FIBERGLASS OR PLASTIC BLADE PADDLES WITH ALUMINUM SHAFTS are extremely durable and maintenance-free. Good fiberglass blade and aluminum shaft paddles will have metal-reinforced tips to keep the fiberglass from wearing and plastic coverings on the shaft for added warmth. Plastic blades can crack if thrown on rocks or stepped on.

BENT SHAFT PADDLES are used for flatwater racing, marathon racing, and canoe tripping. The angle at the throat gives you a more efficient forward stroke. A four- to five-degree angle is good for trips while a twelve- to fifteen-degree angle is best for racing. The more angle you have on your paddle, the more difficult it will be to do a proper J-stroke.

PERSONAL FLOTATION DEVICES (PFDs)

Do not sell yourself short on comfort and quality when buying a PFD (also called a lifevest). Check the label to ensure it is a United States Coast Guard–approved PFD. A

"Type III" is the minimum for recreational boating; a "Type V" has more flotation and is for commercial whitewater use. Try it on. Can you move your arms freely? Will the PFD fit over a bulky sweater as well as adjust to fit snugly over a swimsuit? Does it offer all-day comfort? Can the PFD be secured so that it cannot come off over your head?

Good PFDs are made of closed-cell foam. The old kapok horse-collar lifevests keep your head above water, but the inner compartments can be punctured and absorb water. They are also very uncomfortable to wear (fig. 10).

CANOE CAMPING EQUIPMENT

DULUTH PACKS, first manufactured in Duluth, Minnesota, are the most commonly used packs for wilderness canoe

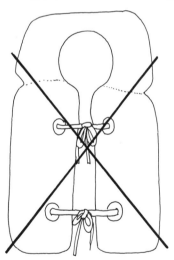
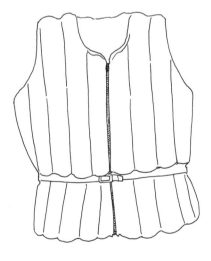

1-10. P.F.D. lifevest

trips. The traditional Duluth packs are made of heavy canvas with leather shoulder straps and *tumplines*. A tumpline strap loops over your forehead and takes some or all the weight off your shoulders. Today these packs are also made of cordura and heavy nylon. Duluth packs, designed to carry a lot of gear, are easy to maneuver in and out of canoes and, with proper care, will last for many years.

RIVER BAGS are waterproof plastic and vinyl sacks with roll-down tops. They come in all sizes, and the larger models have shoulder straps for portaging. They are good insurance to keep your camera, clothing, sleeping bag, and food dry. They are not as durable on long trips as Duluth packs.

PACK BASKETS were traditionally used in the north Maine woods and are still sold by L. L. Bean today. Pack baskets are ideal for carrying dentable items like pots and squashable foods such as bananas and bread. They must be lined with a waterproof sack if you want the contents to stay dry.

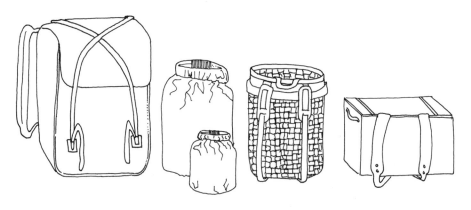

1-11. (Left to right) Duluth pack, river bag, pack basket, and wanigan.

WANIGANS, wooden boxes with tumplines, were commonly used by voyageurs and trappers to carry fragile trade goods. Today wanigans are built of wood, fiberglass, or molded plastic and are used as kitchen boxes to hold pots, eating/cooking utensils, spices, and staples.

2

BASIC
PADDLING TECHNIQUES

YEARS AGO, while waiting for the winds to die down on Telos Lake in northern Maine, we saw a group of paddlers in four canoes headed out across the lake, their canoes overloaded with loose equipment. The paddlers were sitting high on their seats and whipping their paddles from side to side in an attempt to steer. This was inexperience looking for trouble.

Trouble found them when they rounded the point and were hit by the full force of the wind and waves. The second canoe, unable to steer into the wind, was blown broadside to the waves and swamped. The lead canoe turned back to help and capsized. Paddling on the same side, the two paddlers in the third canoe were thrown off balance and went over. The fourth canoe managed to stay upright.

Fortunately it was a warm day, and the wind blew the swimmers, their canoes, and the equipment to shore. In colder water, their inexperience might have cost them far more than the equipment they lost.

Learning to paddle a canoe is similar to learning to ride a bicycle. It takes balance and rhythm. It requires practice, patience, and more practice. But once you invest the time and gain the experience, canoeing can become as easy and effortless as riding a bike.

This chapter will provide a clear and simple overview of strokes used for flatwater canoeing. These same basic strokes are also the foundation for paddling whitewater.

STARTING WITH STYLE

The bow person sits in the *bow* (front) seat; the stern person in the *stern* (back) seat. Find a comfortable position in which your knees are below the gunwales. If your knees stick up over the gunwales, you will have to lift your paddle over them. Shift position from time to time to reduce stiffness in your back and legs: both feet forward, one under your seat, both under your seat, etc.

The bow and stern paddlers should paddle on *opposite*

sides of the canoe to balance the canoe and help it travel in a straight line. Switch sides periodically to reduce muscle fatigue, but do so in unison with your partner. Learn to paddle equally well on both sides right from the beginning. It is also good to switch bow and stern positions. Versatility has many advantages, including increased empathy for your partner's position.

Most of the time you will be sitting in the canoe; however, in high waves and in whitewater, kneel in the canoe, as this lowers your center of gravity and reduces your chances of capsizing. For three-point stability, kneel with your buttocks against the front edge of your seat and spread your knees as wide as possible against the sides of the canoe.

TYPES OF STROKES

In order to develop consistency in canoeing, we will use the same terminology as the American Red Cross and the American Canoe Association.

Canoeing strokes are divided into three groups: *power strokes, turning strokes,* and *braces.*

Power strokes propel the canoe forward or backward.

Turning strokes turn the canoe in a new direction of travel or bring the canoe back on course when it veers off course.

Braces provide stability and are most often used in whitewater.

When you watch experienced paddlers maneuver a canoe up to a dock or down challenging rapids, you will notice they often combine power and turning strokes into one smooth motion. Practice the strokes in their pure forms first. After you get a feel for the canoe and the paddle you will find yourself automatically combining strokes.

PARTS OF THE STROKE

The *plant* is the starting point of a stroke.

The *power* or propulsion phase is the application of force, through the paddle, against the water. This results in movement of the canoe.

The *recovery* phase involves the return of the paddle blade to a plant position. Recoveries involve feathering the blade above the water or slicing the blade through the water.

The *powerface* is the side of the paddle blade which pushes against the water during the forward stroke.

The *backface* is the opposite side or back of the blade. During the back stroke the backface is pushing the water.

Now that you are familiar with paddling terminology, this next section will introduce you to the strokes used in canoeing today. If you are learning strokes for the first time, read through the entire description of the stroke. Then grab your paddle and practice the stroke. Take your time and concentrate on technique, not on speed. Practic-

ing in a canoe is best, but kneeling on the side of a swimming pool or a dock will also work. If you have a video
camera, have someone film you. Then, with book in hand,
watch your video in slow motion and critique your paddling strokes.

STROKES

The Forward Stroke

Within the last decade, the forward stroke has taken on a
new look. There has been a shift from "arm" paddling,
which utilizes smaller, weaker muscles, to "torso" paddling. The torso style of paddling encourages you to use
the stronger and larger muscles of your back, abdomen,
and upper body. Even though this technique may seem
awkward at first it will save you from sore arm muscles on
those long paddling days.

Start on your right side. Slightly rotate your upper body
by moving your right shoulder forward. Keeping both
arms nearly straight, plant your paddle in the water well
ahead of your knees. With your paddle shaft nearly vertical
(figs. 2-1a and 2-1b) uncoil your upper body by driving
your left shoulder forward. Keep your arms straight and
make your shoulders and stomach muscles do the work.
As soon as the paddle reaches your hips, the recovery
phase begins. Slice your blade out of the water and feather
it a few inches above the surface of the water back to the
plant position.

A Plant

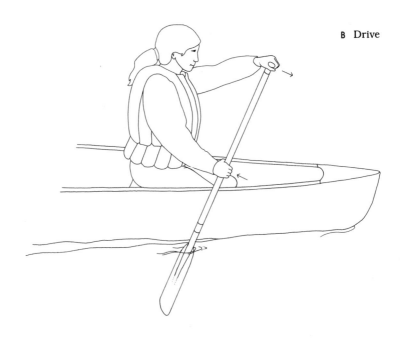

B Drive

C Slice out

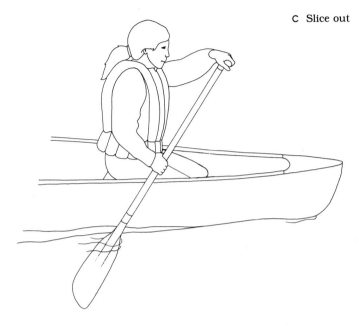

D Recovery

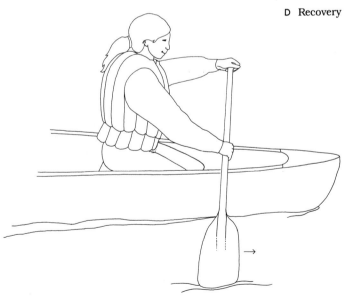

2-1. Forward stroke, side view.

A Plant

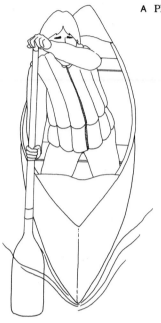

B Drive

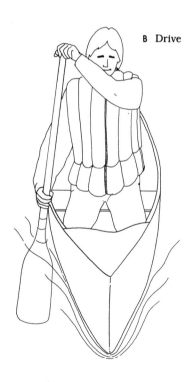

C Slice out

D Recovery

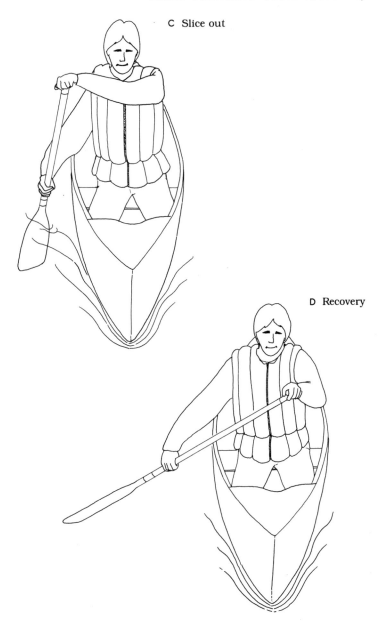

2-2. Forward stroke, front view.

2-3. Poor technique

Key Points:

1. Keep your paddle vertical and not diagonal across your chest during the power phase (fig. 2-3). Your paddle must travel on a line parallel to the center line of your canoe.

2. Keep your torso straight, except for a slight forward lean at the start of the stroke. Excessive forward move-

ment of the upper body will cause the canoe to bob up and down, decreasing your forward momentum.

3. Feather your blade on the recovery phase to reduce wind resistance. There is no need to raise the paddle high above the surface of the water. Relax through the recovery phase.

4. Seventy-five percent of the power in the forward stroke occurs within the first seven inches following the plant. Once the paddle passes your hips there is little forward force applied.

The J-Stroke: Staying on Course

The stern person's stroke causes the canoe to veer off course because he or she sits further from the middle of the canoe. A stern position paddling on the right will cause the canoe to veer left and vice versa. The most elementary stroke used to compensate for this slight deviation is a stern rudder. But as simple as it is, the rudder creates excessive drag and makes paddling in unison difficult. Using a J-stroke will keep the canoe tracking straight without affecting forward speed.

The J-stroke is a forward stroke with a turning stroke added at the end (fig. 2-4c). At the end of each forward stroke, turn the thumb of the top hand down towards the water to turn your blade perpendicular to the water. Give a quick outward hook to provide the corrective push-away force.

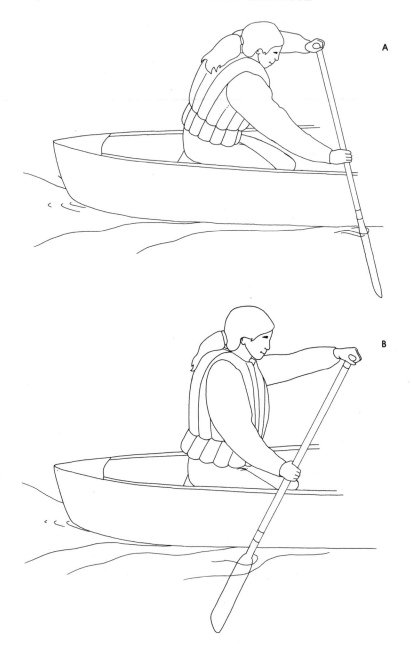

C

2-4. J-stroke.

Key Points:

1. When you start the J-stroke, make sure both your hands are over the gunwale. If the paddle is slightly across your chest your corrective stroke will be ineffective.

2. If your blade is lifting water instead of pushing water, cock the thumb of your top hand further. Your thumb must point to the water to ensure your paddle blade is perpendicular to the surface of the water.

The Back Stroke

The back stroke is used to propel your canoe backward or to decrease forward speed when approaching obstacles such as rocks, moose, or shore.

Plant your paddle in the water next to your hips. With both hands out over the gunwale, use the backface to push water towards the front of the canoe (fig. 5; frame 2-5b and 2-5c). Throughout the power phase of the stroke keep your paddle parallel to the keel line of the canoe. Once the paddle reaches your knees, slice the blade out of the water at a ninety-degree angle to the keel. Rotate the thumb of your top hand forward and feather the blade back to the plant position.

A Reach back and plant

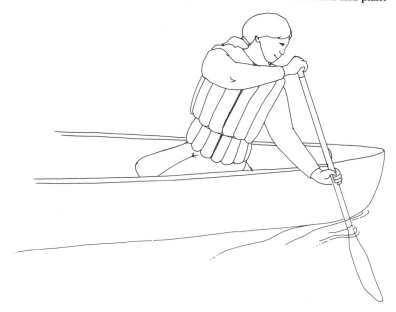

B Flip paddle at hip

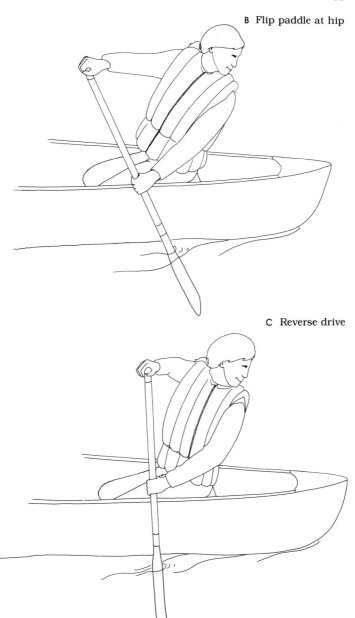

C Reverse drive

2-5. Compound back stroke.

Key Points:

1. Look behind you on your paddling side to see where you are going.

2. Put power into your stroke by using your entire upper body.

3. Make sure your back stroke follows a path parallel to the center line of the canoe.

When traveling backwards, steering the canoe becomes the responsibility of the bow person. This is done by executing a reverse J-stroke at the end of the back stroke. As the blade approaches your knees, turn the thumb of the top hand down towards the water and push water away from the bow. The backface pushes water through the power phase and the reverse J-stroke.

The compound back stroke is a more powerful back stroke. Rotate your upper body so that you can see the stern of the canoe. Reach way back and plant your paddle. With the powerface give a strong, quick pull. Just before the paddle reaches your hips, flip the blade and finish with a normal back stroke. Execute the entire power phase of the compound back stroke on a line parallel to the center line of the canoe.

TURNING STROKES: DRAW, PRY, AND SWEEP STROKES

The Draw

The draw stroke pulls the canoe towards your paddle.

When bow and stern paddlers draw simultaneously (on opposite sides) the canoe spins in a circle.

Start the draw by reaching out with a vertical paddle and plant the blade with the powerface towards you. Extend your top hand as far out as possible to maintain a vertical paddle. Pull your paddle towards the canoe. Just before your paddle reaches the canoe, turn the thumb of the top hand away from the canoe and slice the paddle blade out of the water. Return to the plant position.

2-6. Draw stroke.

Key Points:

1. For a more powerful draw, extend your reach by leaning way out. The draw stroke has a balancing effect on the canoe which allows you to lean out without tipping over. Try it; it works.

2. To gain maximum turning efficiency, perform the draw stroke farthest from the canoe's pivot point. The bow person should finish the stroke at his/her knee while the stern person should finish the stroke just behind himself or herself.

The Cross Draw

The cross draw is performed by the bow paddler to pull the canoe to his/her *off side.* Your off side is the opposite side of the canoe to the one you are paddling on. *Without changing the position of your hands on the paddle,* rotate your upper torso and lift the paddle over and across the bow. Plant the paddle at a forty-five-degree angle to the keel line. Your top hand will be shoulder level and your lower arm will be extended. The power in the cross draw comes when you use your entire torso, not your arms, to pull the paddle to the bow. Keep elbows close to body to prevent shoulder dislocation.

The Pry

The pry pushes the canoe away from your paddle. When done properly a pry is a quick and powerful stroke.

2-7. Cross draw.

The pry involves slicing your paddle under the canoe, doing a quick pry off the side of the canoe, and finishing with an underwater recovery. Start by stretching your top arm out over the water with your thumb pointing towards the stern. Slice the blade under the canoe. Keep your blade deep and your bottom hand just above the gunwale. Pull your top arm towards your nose so the paddle shaft pries off the bilge of the canoe. When your paddle is vertical, stop. Rotate your top hand thumb away from you and slice the blade back under the canoe.

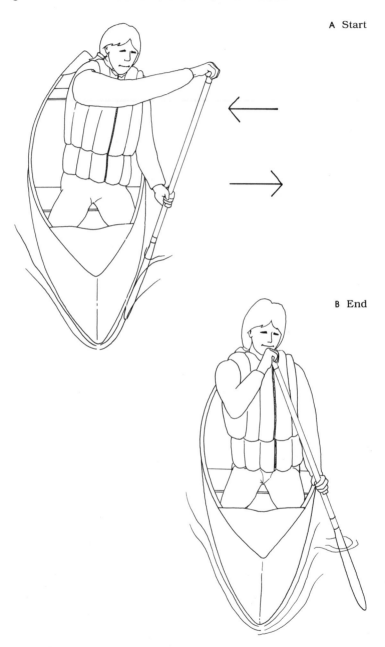

A Start

B End

C Recovery

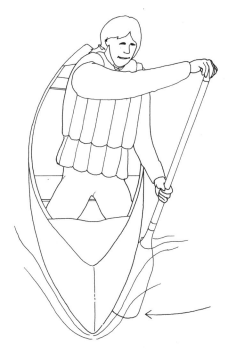

2-8. The pry.

Key Points:

1. Keep your bottom hand above the gunwale or you may catch your thumb between the paddle and the canoe.

2. Keep your top hand well extended over the water at the start.

3. If you are rocking the canoe you are pulling your top hand too far across your chest. This causes your paddle to lift water, forcing the gunwale down.

4. As with the draw, maximum turning efficiency will occur when the stroke is performed farthest from the pivot point.

Sweeps

Sweep strokes are turning strokes in which the paddle "sweeps" the surface of the water in an arch. Sweeps are used in the bow and stern. Although sweeps are not as powerful as the draw and pry, they provide more stability and are useful in shallow water.

The stern forward sweep is used by the stern person to keep the canoe on a straight course. While the J-stroke swings the canoe to your paddling side, the stern forward sweep pushes the canoe away from your paddling side. Begin by extending your paddle out at a forty-five-degree angle and sweep in an arc ending well behind you.

The stern reverse sweep pushes the stern away from your paddling side. Start the stern reverse sweep with your paddle as far back and as close to the stern as possible. Push the water in an arc using the backface of your paddle. Stop the sweep when your paddle is at right angles to the canoe. The most effective part of the stern reverse sweep is the first twelve inches of push-away closest to the stern.

The bow forward sweep will push the bow away from your paddling side. It is good for shallow water and meandering creeks. Plant your paddle as far forward and as close to the bow as possible. Using the powerface of the blade, push the water in an arc. Stop the sweep when the paddle is at right angles to the canoe.

2-9. Forward and reverse sweeps for stern paddler.

2-10. Bow forward sweep.

Key Points:

1. The most effective part all sweep strokes is the push or pull which occurs in the first twelve inches closest to the canoe.

2. Keep your top hand low so your paddle is nearly horizontal.

3. Recover by feathering your blade.

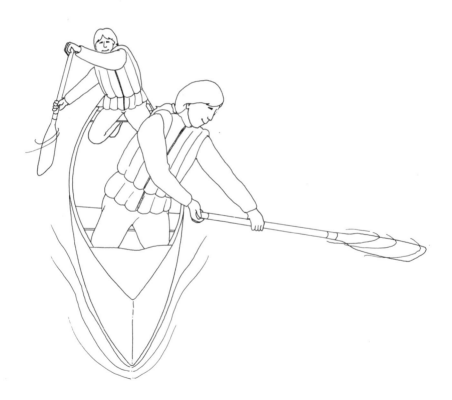

2-11. Stern-high brace and bow-low brace

Braces

Low and high braces are used to prevent a canoe from tipping over and to stabilize a canoe when turning in whitewater. Determining exactly how far you can lean on a brace is best practiced in warm water, close to shore.

Use the low brace when the canoe suddenly tips towards your paddling side. Reach out with a nearly horizontal paddle and place both hands over the water, with your knuckles down. Using the backface, apply a hard and quick downward thrust on the surface of the water. The key points in the low brace are: using a flat blade, a quick slap-push off the water, and both hands out over the water.

The high brace can be used when the canoe tips *away* from your paddling side. This stroke feels as if you're grabbing the water with your paddle to pull yourself upright. It is basically the same as a stationary draw stroke done quickly. The high brace works because of the same righting effect that applies to the draw stroke.

3

LINING, TRACKING, AND PORTAGING

━━━〰〰

Sooner or later you will encounter moving water in the form of ripples, rapids, and falls. Learning to recognize the fun and dangers of moving water will enhance your judgment on deciding whether to wade, line, track, portage, or run (paddle) the rapids. Wading, tracking, and lining are whitewater activities, and there is always a possibility you may slip or the canoe may drag you into the water. It is therefore wise to wear a PFD during these activities.

WADING

Wading is walking your canoe up or down a shallow river. When the river gets too shallow to paddle, you can get out and wade your canoe, lifting it over rocks and guiding it around obstacles. Slippery rocks and dark water will make walking very tricky. Hold on to the canoe decks to maintain your balance. When the current gets too strong to stand up, i.e., over knee-deep, it's time to think of other options.

LINING

Lining is the technique of guiding your canoe down rapids with the use of ropes. Lining is a good option when the rapid is unrunnable and a portage nonexistent. Lining may appear easy, but it is a skill in itself and requires an understanding of river dynamics, some quick thinking, and, when lining with a partner, good communications. Numerous canoes have been damaged or lost while lining because of a lack of skill and judgment.

The downstream painter (bow line) holds the canoe from descending at the same speed as the current. The upstream painter (stern line) is used to *ferry* the canoe around obstacles by *setting* the canoe out into the current or *snubbing* the canoe back towards shore.

To set the canoe out into the current and around a rock, stand slightly upstream of the stern (upstream end in this example) and hold the bow line snug to keep the canoe

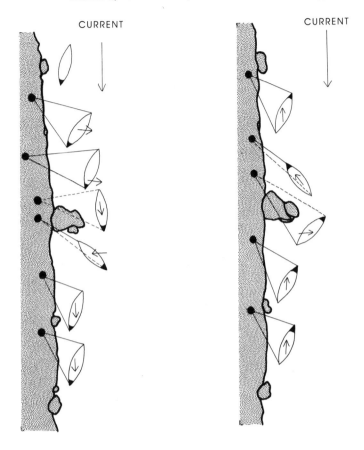

3-1. Lining down a rapid.　　　　3-2. Tracking up a rapid.

from slipping downstream. Gently shove the stern out into the current. Maintain control of the angle of the canoe with the bow and stern lines. In a fast current an angle of ten degrees to the current is about right; in a slow current a forty-five-degree angle will be okay.

The current will push the canoe out towards the middle

of the river. When the stern is clear of the rock, release tension on the bow line and the current will swing the bow parallel to the current. Let the canoe glide past the rock. As the stern drifts past the rock, snub the stern line tight and the canoe will pendulum into shore. Once the canoe comes to a halt, you can hop down the shoreline and continue the process around the next obstacles.

TRACKING

Tracking is pulling your canoe up rapids with the use of ropes. The same concepts used in lining apply in tracking. The upstream painter (bow line) steers the canoe, setting the canoe out into the current or snubbing it back to shore. The downstream line pulls the canoe upstream. Along an unobstructed shoreline you can track your canoe up rapids by pulling it along and maintaining the appropriate angle to keep the canoe away from shore.

When you are lining or tracking, if the angle of the canoe to the current becomes too great, the force of the water against the canoe will drag the person holding the upstream painter into the river. If this happens, release tension on the downstream line, *or* drop the upstream painter and let the boat swing around.

To better understand the river dynamics behind lining and tracking, read the sections in chapter 7, "Introduction to Whitewater," on water reading and ferries.

PORTAGING

Portaging is the art of carrying your canoe and equipment around rapids or falls, from one lake to another, or from one drainage to another. When traveling in very remote areas, take fewer risks running, lining, or tracking rapids, as the consequences of a mishap are greater. Portaging is often the wiser and safer alternative. If you are traveling light you should be able to get over the portage in one trip. If you have to go back for a second load you will be walking the portage trail three times. This turns a two-mile portage into a six-mile portage. On the other hand, carrying heavy loads over difficult terrain is dangerous. The walk back to the start of the trail can be a nice time to pick berries and enjoy the forest.

There are many variations to lifting and carrying canoes. Here are two types of canoe lifts: the solo canoe lift and the assisted canoe lift.

Solo Canoe Lift

Don't let yourself be intimidated by the solo canoe lift. When done correctly it does not require enormous strength. Small people can do this lift.

Here is how to master the solo canoe lift:

1. Stand at the center of the canoe and roll the canoe away from you, up on its side, by lifting the near gunwale.

2. Spread your feet apart for better balance. Bend your knees and, keeping a straight back, lift the canoe up onto your thighs so the inside faces you.

3. With the canoe balanced on your thighs, move your arm that is nearer the bow of the boat across to the far gunwale, and your stern arm between your legs to cradle the canoe.

4. With a rocking motion, swing and roll the canoe up and over your head. Place your head so the canoe yoke lands on your shoulders.

5. Balance the canoe so you can see where you are going. Minor balance adjustments can be made by moving the canoe forward or backward on your shoulders. If the canoe is off balance, tie a PFD or paddle to the stern or bow thwart. A well-balanced canoe is much easier to carry than a poorly balanced canoe.

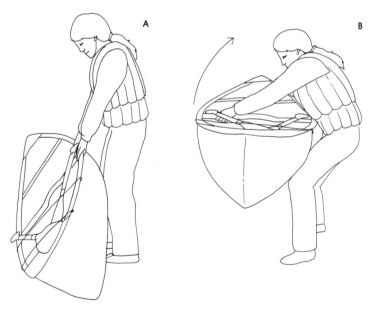

A

B

C

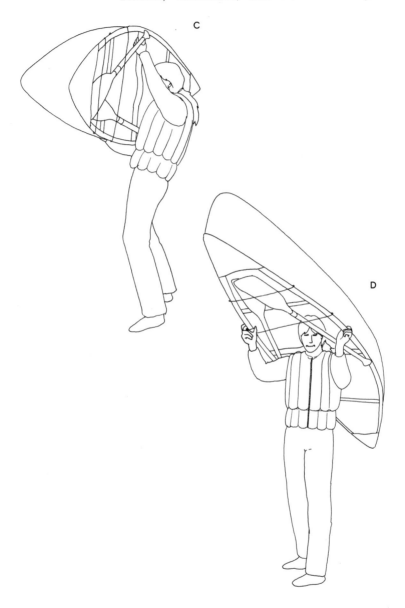

D

3-3. Solo canoe lift.

Assisted Canoe Lift

1. Two people lift *only* the bow of the canoe using the same procedure as the solo canoe lift: up onto the thighs, reach across, swing the canoe up. (The stern of the canoe stays on the ground.)

2. As the helper holds the canoe up over his/her head, the other person ducks under the yoke.

3. To lower the canoe, reverse the order: your partner holds up the bow, you come out from under the yoke and assist in lowering the canoe down onto your laps and then gently down to the ground.

If you wish to change off carrying the canoe without putting it down, get your partner to hold the bow up, while the stern drops to the ground. You can then come out from under the canoe and hold the bow up while your partner slips under the carrying yoke (fig. 4).

If you need a break and do not have a friend within yelling distance, look for a forked tree or a tight clump of trees. Raise the bow up and, with your last ounce of strength, put the canoe into the fork.

Getting across a portage with style takes practice, initiative, and a little stress management. As your adventures lead you down more portage trails, you will solve many of the discomforts and challenges of portaging, such as getting over fallen trees, descending steep banks, crashing through alder thickets, balancing across slippery logs, and moving from rock to rock. Good luck.

3-4. Bridging canoe to trade off.

4

SAFETY

CANOEING, LIKE LIFE, is full of risks. There are obvious risks, such as paddling over a waterfall, and there are less obvious risks, such as paddling on cold and windy lakes. To reduce or avoid risks, first, you must be able to recognize potential dangers: tired and hungry paddlers, cold water, rapids, strong winds, high waves, and lightning storms. Second, you must learn the skills to perform safe rescues in the event of a mishap.

TRAGEDY ON LAKE TIMISKAMING

On June 11, 1978, twenty-seven youths and four adults in four twenty-two-foot Voyageur North canoes headed up Lake Timiskaming on a three-week expedition bound for James Bay. After lunch they set out across the lake, a crossing of approximately one mile. There was a light wind blowing.

As the lead canoe came within 150 yards of shore, it turned broadside to the waves and rolled over. The second canoe dashed to the rescue, turned into the wind, and flipped. The other two canoes paddled to shore to unload their equipment before attempting a rescue. The third canoe was tipped by a panicked swimmer. The fourth capsized while towing a swamped canoe to shore. The offshore winds increased, blowing those in the water out beyond hope. Twelve youths ages twelve to fourteen and one adult died.

How did such a terrible accident happen? What went wrong? Everyone was wearing approved PFDs. They had good equipment and experienced leaders. As we analyze this accident in more detail, you will notice that none of the mistakes they made were life-threatening in themselves. Unfortunately too many mistakes *added up* to create a disaster. In life we all take risks and make mistakes. But we need to recognize when too many risks are *adding up* and leading us towards disaster.

Let's take a closer look at the Lake Timiskaming accident:

RISK #1: *Exhaustion.* After farewell parties, the expedition members left at midnight and drove all night to the put-in.

Be aware of how tired you and your group are. How often have you headed off on a trip very tired and stressed-out from last-minute packing? The excitement of leaving on an expedition can mask how tired you really are.

RISK #2: *Hunger.* After a scant, cold breakfast, the Lake Timiskaming group paddled fifteen miles in four hours. After a quick, light lunch, they paddled on.

It is crucial to eat plenty of food to provide your body with the required calories to paddle all day plus maintain your body's core temperature. Normally you need about two thousand calories a day. To paddle for eight to twelve hours on a cold, rainy day, you may need as many as four thousand calories.

RISK #3: *Out of Shape.* This was the group members' first trip of the season. They had not paddled for eight months.

If you count on getting in shape during the beginning of your trip, adjust your paddling schedule to avoid fatigued muscles. Exhausted bodies do not respond well to emergencies.

RISK #4: *Nonswimmers.* Although all of the Lake Timiskaming group wore approved PFDs, many of the youths could not swim.

Victims of boating accidents are often nonswimmers.

Even while wearing a PFD a nonswimmer is less relaxed in the water. In stressful situations a nonswimmer is less likely to think clearly and perform appropriately.

RISK #5: Poor Weather and Cold Water. The Lake Timiskaming group ventured out on a blustery day with occasional thundershowers. The air temperature was between sixty and seventy-five degrees Fahrenheit, the water temperature fifty degrees.

Cold, wet weather and cold water are often factors in fatal boating accidents. On hot spring days it is easy to forget that the water is cold. Even bright, beautiful mornings can turn wet and cold by afternoon.

RISK #6: Lack of Preparation. The Lake Timiskaming group was unprepared in the event of a dump in cold water. They had not yet practiced a cold-water dump and rescue drill.

Canoes most often capsize in rough waters. The more you practice rescues in controlled situations, the more likely you will be able to effect a fast and safe rescue when your life depends on it.

There are many similarities between the tragedy on Lake Timiskaming and most canoeing fatalities. According to the United States Coast Guard, most boating fatalities include one or more of the following factors:

1. Boaters are not wearing PFDs.
2. People are exposed to cold water and/or cold weather.

---

*Footnote: Facts on the Lake Timiskaming accident were obtained from *The Best of The River Safety Task Force Newsletter,* published by the American Canoe Association.

3. Victims are inexperienced.

4. Alcohol is a contributing factor.

5. Victims are nonswimmers.

The key to preventing a disaster is to be *aware* of *when the risks are adding up* and to reduce or eliminate those risks. For example: Are you tired? Hungry? Cold? Is the weather getting worse? Then it is time to stop paddling, set up camp, build a fire, cook up a warm, hearty meal, and forget about making miles.

PERSONAL FLOTATION DEVICES (PFDs)

Your best insurance for surviving if something goes wrong is your PFD. Put it on *before* you find yourself in cold water with waves breaking over your head. Your PFD works only when properly zipped, with the waist belt snug.

If you are a nonswimmer *always* wear a PFD. Even if you are a good swimmer, in certain situations you should wear your PFD. Put your PFD on when you are wearing heavy clothing which will drag you down (rain gear, rubber boots, big sweaters). You should also wear your PFD in the following situations: when the water temperature is below sixty degrees Fahrenheit; paddling in high wind and waves; paddling at night; paddling in whitewater; paddling alone. Be sure to invest in a comfortable PFD so that you will enjoy wearing it.

RESCUES

Rescuing Yourself

Warm-Water Self-Rescue

If you capsize in *warm water,* tow or paddle your canoe to shore. Grab hold of the painter or the deck of your canoe and with strong side strokes tow the canoe to shore. If you are a poor swimmer, you may find it faster to right the canoe, sit in the bottom of the swamped canoe, and paddle to shore.

Canoes differ in the ways they float when they are full of water. Some float below the surface while others float higher. Some after swamping turn right side up, others stay upside down. Take your canoe for a swim and learn how it responds. Practice towing a swamped canoe one hundred yards. It is not as easy as you might think.

Cold-Water Self-Rescue

If you capsize in *cold water,* you must make a quick and crucial decision whether to strike out for shore or to wait for a rescue. A high number of canoeing fatalities are the result of being dumped in cold water. If you have ever fallen in ice-cold water, you know what a shock it is. It takes your breath away! Act quickly before hypothermia reduces blood flow to the brain and your decision-making ability becomes impaired.

If you dump in cold water and there is little chance of a rescue, you must abandon your canoe and head for shore as quickly as possible. Check which way the wind will blow you and head for the closest shore.

If a rescue is on the way it is best to reduce heat lost by using the *HELP* or *huddle* position. According to the Red Cross, both the HELP and huddle positions can increase your cold water survival time by fifty percent.

HELP position (Heat Escape Lessening Position): floating in your PFD, bring your knees up to your chest and tuck your arms in close to your side. Keep your head above water since a wet head can rob you of vital body heat at a rapid rate.

If you are in cold water with other swimmers, form a "huddle" while waiting for a rescue. Wrap your arms and legs around each other and huddle close together without moving. The huddle can only be done with the aid of PFDs. If young children are involved, they should be placed in the center of the huddle as they lose heat more rapidly than adults.

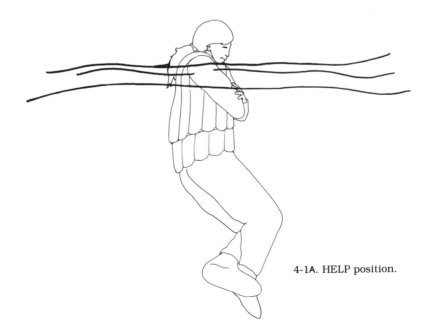

4-1A. HELP position.

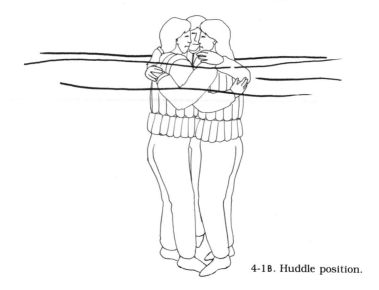

4-1B. Huddle position.

Rescuing Swimmers

Towing Swimmers

There are numerous ways to tow swimmers to shore. We recommend you tow them with the canoe's stern painter or have them hold onto the stern of your canoe. It's hard work to tow a swimmer, so tell him or her to help by kicking his or her feet, or a towed swimmer can decrease body drag by wrapping his or her legs around the stern of your canoe.

Be careful how you approach a panicky swimmer, as he or she may grab the side of your canoe and tip you.

Getting Swimmers into a Canoe

When the water is cold, get swimmers out of the water quickly. Getting a swimmer into your boat is tippy busi-

4-2. Rescuing swimmers.

ness. The safest method is to have a second canoe come up parallel to your canoe. The paddlers in the other canoe can stabilize your canoe by holding onto your gunwale. Allow your canoe to tip a little on the swimmers' side so they don't have to climb as high. The swimmers should kick, pull, and roll their bodies into your canoe (fig. 4e).

If there is no other canoe to help, have the swimmers climb in from one end while you sit on the bottom, in the middle of the canoe, to lower the center of gravity. Practice in a pool or at the beach on a warm, sunny day.

Rescuing Canoes

When you are close to shore, you can tow a swamped canoe behind you. Pick up the painter of the swamped canoe and wrap it around your thwart. Paddle *hard*—a seventeen-foot canoe full of water weighs approximately 3,225 pounds.

Canoe Over Canoe Rescue

This maneuver is used to get water out of a swamped canoe by pulling it up and over the rescue canoe. First, check the swimmers. If they are cold, get them out of the water. If they are not cold, they can assist with the rescue from the water.

Paddle to one end of the swamped canoe. Meet your partner in the center of the canoe, face each other, and kneel down to keep your center of gravity low. Grab the end of the swamped canoe, lift it up on your gunwale, and turn it upside down. Now swing the canoes into a T pattern. Pull the swamped canoe up and across your canoe. Finally, when both ends are clear of the water, flip the canoe right side up and slide it back into the water.

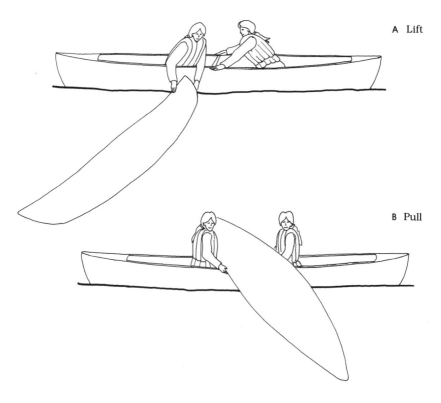

A   Lift

B   Pull

C Flip

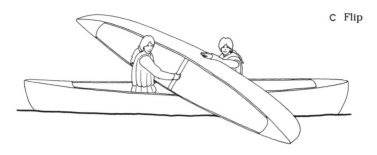

D Return

E Swimmers climb in

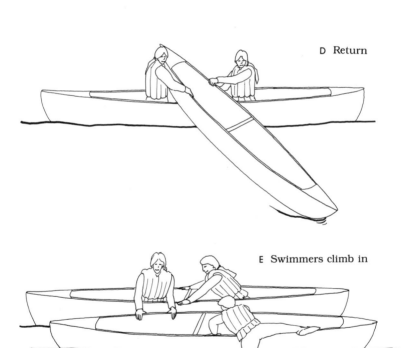

4-3. Canoe-over-canoe rescue.

Key Points:

1. It's difficult to lift a swamped canoe up onto your gunwale. It helps if you roll the canoe onto its side before you attempt to lift the end. This breaks the suction if it is upside down or pours the water out if it is right side up.

2. Get the swimmers to help you. One swimmer can help get the canoe up on the gunwale by pushing down on the far end of the swamped canoe. The second swimmer can help keep the canoes in a T pattern.

3. When the wind is blowing, swimmers should never let go of one of the canoes during the rescue. Canoes can be blown across a lake faster than a person can swim.

HYPOTHERMIA

Hypothermia is a lowering of the body's temperature, resulting in impaired muscle and brain functions. When people are hypothermic, their bodies are losing heat faster than they can produce it. The two types of hypothermia are mild hypothermia and severe hypothermia. *You must be able to differentiate between these two levels of hypothermia, as the treatments are nearly opposite.*

Mild Hypothermia

It is much easier to prevent hypothermia than to treat it. Therefore, recognizing the events leading up to it is critical. Let's say your friend did not sleep well last night because mosquitoes got in the tent. The oatmeal was slightly burnt, so he did not eat any breakfast. The rain soaked through his cheap rain gear, and his wet cotton clothing conducted vital body heat away. All morning he kept warm by paddling hard. But by noon he was exhausted, hungry, *cold,* and suffering from mild hypothermia.

If your friend is suffering from mild hypothermia, he will be cold, unmotivated, and lethargic. He will shiver, have difficulty with finger coordination (like undoing buttons), and his paddling strokes will become sluggish and slow. At this point, he is losing more heat than his body can produce, and he must be treated immediately.

First, *prevent further heat loss.* Get him out of the cold water, rain, or wind. Take his wet clothes off and replace them with dry clothes. Second, help his body generate more heat. Refuel him with high-energy foods such as chocolate bars, granola bars, or candies, and give him a hot drink. Get him moving around and doing isometrics. If he is unwilling to do the above, place him in a warm sleeping bag and add external heat to his core with hot water bottles or warm stones, or sandwich him between two warm bodies.

If your friend slides into severe hypothermia, do none of the above.

Severe Hypothermia

Unless you carry a special rectal thermometer which registers body temperatures below eighty degrees Fahrenheit, you will have to rely on observation of external signs to diagnose severe hypothermia. The most common signs are: shivering stops, pulse and respiration slow down, and speech becomes incoherent. Coordination will deteriorate to the point where walking is difficult, and a progressive loss of consciousness will follow. The sooner you recognize the seriousness of this condition and start treatment, the better the chances of survival.

Prevent further heat loss and *handle the victim very gently.* There is a buildup of toxic wastes and lactic acid in the blood in the body's extremities. Movement or rough handling will cause a flow of blood from the extremities to the core. This polluted blood can send the heart into ventricular fibrillation. Whatever you do, handle the person very gently. Do not give any food or drink as this may cause vomiting. Don't try to rewarm the victim in the field. Wrap the victim in a couple of sleeping bags and insulate him/her from the ground. Place some warm water bottles under the armpits and in the groin area to help maintain body temperature. Establish an evacuation plan to get the person to a medical facility as soon as possible.

PUTTING IT ALL TOGETHER

A number of years ago I (Matty) was leading an Outward Bound group on an extended canoe expedition in northern Ontario. As we approached Whitewater Lake, I instructed the students to put on their PFDs, paddle close to shore, and stay together, since this lake is notorious for high winds and cold water. After lunch, the wind picked up slightly. We decided to keep paddling and designated a lead canoe and a sweep canoe.

About an hour later I heard "canoe over." The two swimmers grabbed onto the bow and stern of the first canoe which reached them. I pulled up parallel to the rescue canoe, had them steady my canoe, and assisted the swimmers into my canoe. I headed to shore with the swimmers and another canoe. My partner and the other two canoes stayed out to rescue the swamped canoe and the packs. When we arrived on shore we exchanged wet clothes for dry ones, set up a tent, started a fire, and fed the swimmers warm soup and hot drinks. The rest of the group soon arrived and joined us for soup.

This rescue took less than ten minutes. The swimmers were out of the water in four minutes. Because we had practiced rescues earlier in the course, everybody knew what to do, and very few words were spoken.

Safety management is not dictated by rules. There are no rules that apply all the time. What does apply is good judgment. Good judgment is based on *awareness, intuition, foresight, skill,* and *experience.*

Awareness. Are you tired? Hungry? Are there non-swimmers in your group? What is the weather doing? Did your partner not sleep well last night or not eat lunch? How cold is the water? Are you *aware* of what is going on around you?

Intuition. Listen to your gut feelings and act upon them: "I don't *feel* good about paddling in these big waves!" "I think the group is getting tired."

Foresight. The *"what if"* questions: "The wind is blowing us away from shore. If I dump here I will get blown out." "I'm tired, and the portage trail is wet and slippery. If we portage now I am more likely to slip." Play out different scenarios in your head—*before* the worst happens!

Skills. Do you have the skills to rescue yourself and your friends? To paddle in strong winds? To read a map and determine how far the next waterfall is? Know your limitations.

Learn to recognize *when the risks are adding up.*

5

TRIP PLANNING

INITIAL PLANNING

IMAGINE THAT THREE FRIENDS and yourself have decided to take a few weeks off this summer to paddle a river in northern Ontario.

First, how much time do you and your friends have for the trip?

"Three weeks," you say.

What is your budget?

"We can't afford to fly in or out but can drive a day or two."

What type of a trip do you want: challenging, relaxing, fishing, remote?

"A scenic river trip through fairly remote wilderness area. Challenging but not nerve-racking."

What is your group's overall paddling ability?

"We have done a number of weekend trips around Minnesota, and two of us took an intermediate whitewater course at Madawaska Kanu Camp last summer."

Here are the steps you must take to set your paddling adventure in motion. Get yourself a map of northern Ontario. A road map will do. Notice that most of the lake and river systems flow either south into Lake Superior or north to James Bay or Hudson Bay. The rivers which flow into Lake Superior can be accessed by Trans-Canada Highway #17. They are about a hundred miles in length and in most cases would require paddling the shore of Lake Superior to get to a roadhead for a take-out. Since you are looking for a longer trip, take a look at the rivers flowing north. These look about the right length for a two- to three-week trip. Since you can't afford to fly out, you will have to paddle a river that ends in Moosonie, where you can catch the train back to Cochrane. This narrows down your options to the Missinaibie, Groundhog, Mattagami, Frederickhouse, and Abitibi rivers.

The second step is to get as much information as possible for the options you've picked. Call or write local canoe outfitters, canoe rental companies, and outdoor equipment stores and ask for books or route descriptions on the rivers you are interested in. Write to local paddling clubs.

They too have a wealth of information and can often refer you to someone who has paddled the river. Try the Chamber of Commerce in the largest town near the start of your river trip. For best results, enclose a self-addressed, stamped envelope. Keep your questions to a minimum and welcome collect calls.

Maps

Once you've gathered enough information, it is time for your group to choose a river and purchase large-scale maps. Order topographic maps to ensure that the rapids and falls will be marked. The 1:250,000 scale is often used for canoeing maps. It is always an exciting moment when the maps arrive. You can begin to visualize, in more detail, what lies ahead.

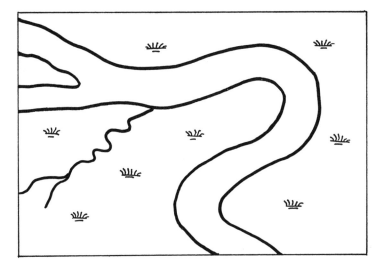

5-1. This map shows a slow-moving river winding through a swampy area. Campsites might be poor, but it is a good area to see wildlife.

What Is a Topographic Map?

A topographic map is a map which uses contour lines to indicate topography, i.e., the ups and downs of the terrain. The contours show a continuous line of elevation, bending into valleys and bulging out around ridges. If you follow along a contour line on your map you will come to a number. This number indicates, in feet or meters, the elevation above sea level that this line represents. The elevation difference between each contour line can be found on the bottom of the map. If your map indicates one-hundred-foot contours, this means that there is one hundred feet of elevation difference between one contour line and the next. Where the contour lines run close together the terrain will be very steep, and where they are far apart the terrain will have a gentle slope.

Getting Information from Your Map

Lay all your maps out on the floor. Check the map's scale at the bottom. On a 1:250,000 map, one inch will equal four miles. Starting at your put-in, mark off every inch (or more, depending on scale) with a bright dot and write in the appropriate mileage, i.e., 4, 8, 12 and so on. The best way to accurately mark mileage on a map is to use a small string marked off with a pen mark at every inch. Carefully place the string on the map following each bend in the river and place a mark on the map adjacent to the mark on the string. Every time a contour line crosses the river, mark it with a red arrow. Also, mark waterfalls in red. Highlight marked portages and also road access since the

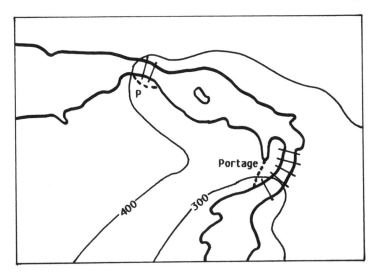

5-2. There is a one-hundred-foot drop between the first and third lakes, which probably indicates waterfalls! Both portages are on river right. The end of the portage might be a good place to camp, to fish in the pool below the falls.

latter can serve as possible communication or evacuation points.

You now have fairly accurate river miles for your trip. You can also calculate the slope of specific river sections by dividing river drop by distance. Take a look at fig. 3. Between mile markers 75 and 80 two contour lines cross the river. The total drop is one hundred feet in a five-mile section: one hundred divided by five equals twenty feet per mile. As a general rule you can expect a river with a gradient of five to ten feet per mile to be good cruising, with some rapids or falls. A river with a gradient of ten to thirty feet per mile might offer challenging and runnable whitewater or hazardous falls. Rivers with drops of fifty feet or more per mile are out of the question for loaded tripping canoes and will require portaging.

Itinerary

Studying and marking the maps as outlined above will help you prepare your trip itinerary. A trip itinerary is simply a tentative schedule. If you come across a beautiful campsite, stop even though you have not covered the day's miles. On the other hand, if you arrive at your designated campsite and the group is not tired, put in a few extra miles to get ahead of schedule. As long as you don't get too far ahead of or behind your itinerary, you'll be fine.

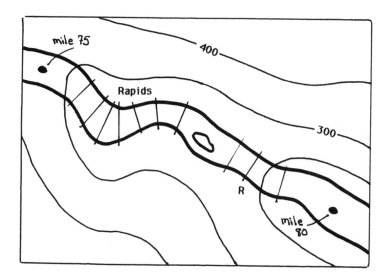

5-3. Contour lines indicate that the river runs through a canyon. Between miles 75 and 80, the river drips 100 feet in five miles. This could mean that all or some of the rapids are runnable, depending upon the water level and your canoeing ability.

Sat./ 12	Sun / 13	mon./ 14	Tues./ 15	Wed / 16	Thurs./ 17
	L D	B L D	B L D	B L D	B L
Drive to State Park Shuttle cars to take-out	6 miles 2 portages	10 miles 3 portages	8 miles 1 portage ½ day Lay-over at Falls	15 miles 0 portages	12 miles 2 portages Drive Home
▲ State Park	▲ Long Lake	▲ Big Bend	▲ Cedar Falls	▲ Nip Lake	Home!

5-4. B, L, D = Breakfast, lunch, dinner to be eaten on the trail A = campsite for that night

Some key points to remember when planning an itinerary:

1. In ideal conditions (no wind, no portages, and the group is in good condition) you can plan to paddle three miles an hour. With three to four hours of paddling in the morning and three in the afternoon, you will average about twenty miles per day. Use twenty miles per day as a guideline for planning mileage.

2. Be conservative in your mileage for the first few days to allow muscles to adjust to the extra work.

3. For river sections where you have numerous portages or runnable rapids, don't plan to cover twenty river miles a day. On less-traveled routes, portage trails can be hard to find. If you have to make two trips across the portage to get all your equipment over, you will walk three times the distance. Scouting rapids also takes time.

4. If you want to fish at the bottoms of rapids, pick berries, enjoy long leisurely lunches with friends, or

start paddling at the break of day, plan your itinerary accordingly.

5. We encourage you to plan at least one layover day (rest day) per week to allow for sore muscles, bad weather, superb fishing, or illness/injury.

Menu Planning

Now that you have your itinerary done, your next most important task is to prepare a menu and pack your food. Numerous expeditions have not succeeded because of a lack of good, nutritious food. A delicious, simple, and well-prepared dinner will do more than anything else to bring morale up at the end of a rainy day.

Menu planning and food packing can be inexpensive and fun. Best are simple, hearty meals that are easy to cook, supplemented with a good spice kit and a few exotic treats such as Swiss chocolate, Camembert cheese, and baked bread every few days. Many of the foods you eat at home (oatmeal, pancakes, dry soups, noodles, rice) are well suited for the trail. You will find most of the ingredients you need at your local health food store.

On your trip itinerary, for each day mark *B* for breakfast, *L* for lunch, and *D* for dinner to indicate each meal you plan to eat on the trail.

Here is a sample menu for a two-week trip:

Breakfasts

The input your receive from the group might include suggestions like pancakes only on layover days since they take so long to cook, no cornmeal or sardines, no more than one-third cooked breakfasts, and lots of brown sugar for the oatmeal. Here is a sample breakfast menu:

1 pancakes for layover day
3 oatmeal with raisins, dried apples, and cinnamon
5 granola (different types) with powdered milk
2 muesli
2 raisin bran with stewed fruit

___

13 TOTAL

Lunches

The group decides to: not plan hot lunches but bring extra soup mix for hot soup on cold, rainy days; eat bread from home only for the first two to three days; bake trail bread every third day; eat dried fruit instead of fresh fruit to keep packs light. The group decides to pack lunches in three stuff sacks: breads; cheeses and meat; and snacks. At lunch you will pull out one item from each bag.

BREAD STUFF SACK:

1 rye bread (from home)
1 bagel (from home; 1½ per person)
1 pita bread (from home; 2 per person)
4 lunches of assorted crackers
4 lunches of flapjacks (homemade granola bars)
3 lunches of bread baked on the trail (2 bannock, 1 cornbread)

___

14 TOTAL

CHEESE AND MEAT STUFF SACK:

>   6 lunches of cheese (1 gouda, 2 cheddar, 1 cream
>   cheese, 2 swiss)
>   4 salami
>   2 sardines
>   2 beef jerky
>   _____
>   14 TOTAL

SNACK STUFF SACK (2 snacks per day × 14 days = 28 snacks):

>   — sugar treats: hard candy, chocolate bars, fruitcakes
>   — dried fruit: raisins, dates, apples, prunes, figs,
>   pineapple, pears, peaches, fruit leather
>   — salty treats: peanuts, mixed nuts, gorp, corn nuts,
>   sesame sticks

Dinners

Dinner requests include fresh food on the first night out, with the rest to be prepacked individual dinners which are reasonably light but hearty. To keep planning simple you choose a four-day rotation.

>   1 first night: steak, baked potatoes, and a fresh salad
>   3 macaroni and cheese
>   3 spaghetti
>   3 curried rice
>   3 lentil stew
>   _____
>   13 TOTAL

Drinks	Condiments
— hot chocolate	— margarine/butter
— tea	— oil (to fry your fish)
— coffee	— spice kit
— sugar	— popcorn
— powdered milk	— peanut butter
— juice crystals	— jams

To ensure your food is waterproof, double bag each individual meal and pack meals into their appropriate stuff sacks. But first, line each stuff sack with one or two large, heavy-duty plastic bags.

CAMPING EQUIPMENT AND CLOTHING

Don't run down to your local outdoor store to buy all the latest in outdoor clothing and camping equipment. Look around your basement or garage, dig through your old clothing, and talk to friends. You might just find what you need or be able to borrow a missing piece of equipment.

The following is a sample list of equipment for a twelve-day river trip where the intention is to paddle as much whitewater as possible, so some of the equipment and clothing will reflect that.

Equipment

First Aid Kit: An adequate but simple first aid kit, well waterproofed and easily accessible

Paddles: 2 laminated wood paddles and 2 fiberglass paddles for whitewater

Packs: 1 Duluth pack for food and equipment; 1 waterproof river bag for clothing and sleeping bags; 1 ammo box for camera and journal

Tent: One freestanding dome tent, with a good rain fly

Sleeping Pad: Ensolite pad or a Therma-Rest

Sleeping Bag: Three-season fiberfill bags put into stuff sacks and lined with heavy plastic bags

Clothing Sack: A stuff sack lined with a heavy plastic bag for extra clothing

Cook Stove: Optimus-8R with a half-gallon of fuel (we used the stove when raining or to cook in the tent when the bugs were ferocious)

Cook Pots: Medium and small size nesting stainless steel pots with "scrubbie" for cleaning, packed in garbage bag so that fire-blackened pots didn't blacken everything in the pack

Reflector Oven: A camping reflector oven for baking bread and desserts

Eating Tools: Two hard plastic mugs, wooden bowls, spoons, and Swiss army knives

Matches: Packed in a small watertight container plus a couple of lighters

Map and Compass: A small Silva compass, one set of 1:250,000 topo maps, and a Ministry of Natural Resources river map

Clothing

Footwear and socks:
1 pair running shoes or the like for paddling, with wool socks
1 pair camp boots or shoes for camp

Paddling clothes:
Loose fitting pants and loose, long-sleeved shirt
Bandana and sun hat
Paddling jacket and rain pants (for whitewater)

Rain Gear:
Coated or rubberized nylon jacket and pants
Poggies or waterproof work gloves for hands

Extra Clothes:
2–3 pairs polypropylene or wool socks
1 pair polypropylene or wool underwear (top and bottom)
1 pile or wool jacket
1 wool sweater
1 wool hat

Toiletries:
Toothbrush, paste, lip balm, insect repellent, etc.

PACKING AND WATERPROOFING

Murphy's law: "If you don't waterproof your food and equipment, it will get wet." So waterproof your stuff unless, of course, you want to have one of those epic trips which you've read about: "We wrung out our sleeping bags and attempted to dry them around the fire in the pouring rain. Our food was beyond hope; the cans of tuna were okay, but the macaroni was a glob of gluten."

Good river bags are the best insurance for keeping food, clothing, and equipment dry. Another method of waterproofing is to buy or make a bunch of nylon stuff sacks and line them with heavy-duty plastic bags. The plastic bag must be inside the stuff sack to protect it from getting ripped. Pack your food, clothing, and anything else you want to keep dry in them. Squeeze all the air out of the plastic bag and twist and tie the top. Mark your stuff sacks so they are easy to identify: breakfast, dinner, clothes, etc. Using different colored stuff sacks also helps. Stuff sacks are then packed into canoe packs (See chapter 1, "Equipment").

First aid kits and cameras are best packed in ammunition boxes or waterproof plastic boxes. Ammunition boxes can be found at your nearest army surplus outlet.

CANOEING WITH CHILDREN

Children love to be included in family canoe trips. When canoeing with children, be it an hour-long paddle down the lake or a weekend canoe camping trip, the essential element is *fun*. Children dislike being stuffed into uncomfortable PFDs, told to sit still in the canoe for hours, and constantly asked to keep their shoes dry. When children are not having a good time, they make sure that no one else is having a good time either. To ensure a safe and fun experience, let's go over safety concerns for young ones, adapting to the needs of children, and canoe camping with kids.

Safety

For starters, each child needs a good, comfortable PFD which fits properly. Check the tag in the PFD to make certain it is United States Coast Guard–approved and will support the weight of your child. Try the lifevest on the child. It should be able to adjust to fit snugly over a T-shirt or a few layers of sweaters and a raincoat. Children's life vests should have a crotch strap to keep the vest from slipping off over their heads. Once you've invested in a good PFD you need to make it clear to the child why he or she must wear the lifevest at all times around the water. Explain to your child that the lifevest must be worn properly, with the zipper up, the waist belt snug and the crotch strap done up. It is a good idea to test the PFD to see how well it floats your child. To emphasize the importance of wearing a lifevest you should set an example by wearing yours.

The next safety consideration is appropriate clothing to protect children from sun, wind, rain, and cold. Sunburn on a small child can be very serious. Cover up exposed skin with long-sleeve shirts and pants, shade faces with sun hats and visors, and use waterproof sunblock lotion (30 or higher). Bring lots of extra clothes to protect against wind, rain, and cold. Children, because of their small body masses, are more susceptible to cold. If they do not have good rain gear, supplement with a poncho, tarp, or umbrella. It is a good idea to bring many changes of clothes as some children make it a habit to get wet. Tender little feet need protection from sharp rocks, rusty fishing hooks, and broken glass. An old pair of sneakers is ideal for wading into unknown waters.

Adapting to the Needs of Children

Having a fun trip may mean adjusting your expectations, adapting your canoeing style, and creatively involving your children in the adventure. Sitting still in the bottom of the canoe for a long time gets monotonous. Children enjoy hanging their hands overboard, throwing things in the water, towing a toy boat, or trying their luck at fishing. Even at a young age, they will want to help paddle. Look for a lightweight paddle, about their own height. Have them sit on a pack or kneel close to the side of the canoe. Offset their weight with a pack on the opposite side.

Children have short attention spans and boundless energy. Plan your trips with numerous stops to stretch, run around, and explore. Bring along a basket of easy-to-munch-on snacks so that children can help themselves when they get hungry and thirsty. Nap time in the canoe can be fun. Make a bed by lining the canoe with ensolite pads and use tarps to protect children from sun, wind, or rain.

Canoe Camping with Children

Overnight canoe camping trips with children are great fun. Unlike backpacking, where *you* have to carry all of their extra paraphernalia, there is always room for the essential teddy bear, favorite blanket, and nighttime storybook.

When camping with children, bring a large tent so your kids have a place to play when the mosquitoes are bad or when the weather turns nasty. Make sure your tent has a good, waterproof rain fly and no-see-um netting.

The best way to keep children out of trouble around camp is to keep them involved. Have them help set up the tent, collect firewood, build the fire, and wash their own cups and spoons. Children love to cook their own food too, so don't forget the hot dogs and marshmallows.

Like moths, children are drawn to campfires. Take time to explain fire safety and ensure that there is no clutter around the fire where a child could trip and fall into the fire.

Some kids are afraid of the dark, especially in strange places. It may help to give them their very own flashlight. Never leave children in a tent with a candle. A nylon tent can go up in flames in less than minute.

Canoeing with children can be a very enjoyable and rewarding family activity. As your children grow, your outings will get longer and more adventurous. Before long they will be asking to borrow the car and the canoe to head off on their own.

6

WIND, WAVES
AND LIGHTNING

THE FORCES OF WIND, waves, and lightning cannot be "conquered." To fight these forces of nature is foolish and often ends in disaster.

WIND AND WAVES

Lakes both large and small have the potential for wind and waves. As a general rule, winds increase through the day and die down in the evening. In this case, you are wise to rise at dawn, paddle until the winds increase, lay over for the day, and paddle again in the evening.

Sometimes the winds on large lakes will calm only at night. Paddling by starlight or moonlight is possible when the lake is smooth as glass, the sky clear, and the route easy to navigate. When you paddle at night, wear your lifevest. Paddle close to shore so if a wind blows up, you can get off the lake quickly.

Winds on lakes are classified as headwinds, tailwinds or crosswinds. In a headwind you will be paddling directly into the wind. A tailwind blows from behind you. A crosswind blows against the side of your canoe. Each type of wind requires a different technique.

Before battling headwinds, study your map for possible windbreaks and resting points. These may include the leeward shoreline, islands, or points of land. Plot a route which offers you the most wind protection and options for getting off the lake if the wind does increase (fig. 6-1).

When you paddle into headwinds with large waves, you may need to lighten the bow so it rises over the waves and takes in less water. This can be accomplished by shifting the packs towards the stern or putting the lighter paddler in the bow. Too light a bow is also a problem in headwinds as a light bow may catch the wind and be blown off course.

Skill is required to hold a canoe on course while heading into the wind. To ensure forward progress, both paddlers need to paddle hard with the stern paddler executing quick and effective correction strokes. If the stern paddler rudders, not only does he or she miss forward strokes, but

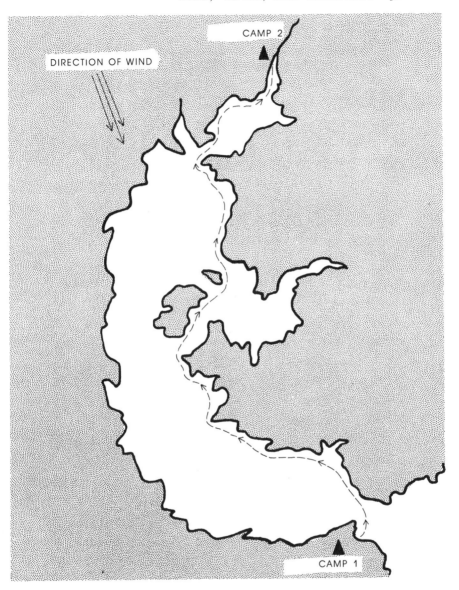

6-1. Route from camp 1 to camp 2 uses leeward shoreline.

the dragging paddle slows the forward momentum of the canoe.

As waves increase in size and speed, the top of the wave curls over. This is called a breaking wave. Sometimes the so-called "seventh wave" will be a breaking wave. Watch out for these. As the breaking wave approaches, turn the bow straight into it or ten degrees off. You will lose forward speed, but pushing straight into the wave reduces your chance of being rolled over or taking water in over the side. Whitecaps occur when a strong wind has whipped up a lake full of breaking waves. It is a clear sign to get off the lake.

Paddling crosswinds requires another set of tactics. Even in a light crosswind, you will be blown sideways, arriving downwind of your desired destination. As crosswinds and waves increase, the risk of taking in water and being rolled over by the waves also increases. To avoid these problems you will need to *quarter the waves*. This term refers to cutting an angle through the waves. In a light wind this can be a large angle, for example, fifty degrees. In a strong wind one needs a smaller angle, such as fifteen degrees.

To cross from point to point (fig. 6-2) you need to set about a forty-five-degree angle to the wind. Remember to turn the bow into the occasional large breaking wave to keep from taking in water.

You may think paddling a tailwind is simple. This is true in light winds, but as wind and waves increase, tailwinds become more challenging. As the wave comes from behind you, it pushes the stern up, and the canoe starts to pick up speed as it surfs down the face of the wave and buries its bow in the wave ahead. As the wave passes under the canoe, it tries to pivot the canoe sideways into the trough created between the two waves. If this happens,

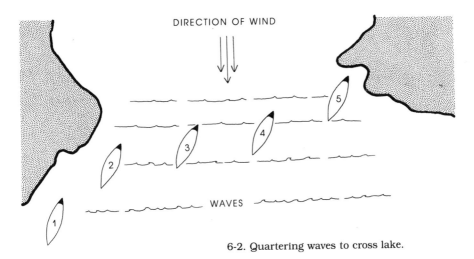

DIRECTION OF WIND

WAVES

6-2. Quartering waves to cross lake.

you may find yourself in the water. To keep the canoe from turning into the trough, use a strong rudder or a draw.

Practice paddling big waves on warm days with an onshore wind blowing. If you capsize, the wind will blow you and your canoe into shore. This practice will give you first-hand experience with just how big a wave you and your canoe can safely handle.

Canoeing groups often find it difficult to stay together on windy lakes. The best plan of action is to designate an experienced paddler to stay in the lead. The lead boat can set the pace, demonstrate the necessary quartering angle, choose a safe route close to shore, and call rest stops as needed. It's also a good idea to have an experienced "sweep" boat to bring up the rear and be ready to help paddlers who are having difficulty. If there are no rest stops, wait for slower paddlers by pointing your canoe into the wind and paddling just hard enough to hold your position.

One way to keep a group together on a windy lake, when the wind is not too strong, is to raft up. Rafting up involves tying canoes side by side. Canoes lashed together become virtually impossible to tip over. Use extreme caution when tying canoes together, as the canoes become less mobile and can easily be swamped. One disadvantage—and a cause for real caution in using this technique—is that rafted canoes are at greater risk of taking in water, especially the canoe on the windward side. Since the canoe is unable to rock over the waves, water will splash in over the side. This problem can be reduced by quartering waves or reducing the weight in the windward canoe to increase its freeboard. In a headwind, waves will splash up between the canoes, and water will come in behind the bow seat. This can be avoided by lashing the canoes two feet apart at midship.

The easiest place to build a raft is on a flat beach. Find strong poles and place them across the center thwart, stern thwart, and behind the bow seat. Check that canoes are about two feet apart at midship and that the bows and sterns are the same distance apart. With painters or extra rope tightly lash the poles.

Remember: tying canoes together should only be done by experts familiar with the technique and aware of the hazards involved.

Sailing

Occasionally you will be lucky and have a stiff breeze blowing your way. Your imagination will become obsessed with how to harness this power. At first you try holding up your poncho, then as your arms get tired you tie the top corners of the poncho to the tops of two paddles. Now you are really sailing. But bigger is better. Dig out your kitchen tarp, ground sheet, or tent fly and cut eight- to twelve-foot poles to replace the paddles. Tie the tops of the poles back to the stern thwart. The stern person steers this vessel by using his/her paddle as a rudder. Sailing a single canoe with a lot of sail is very tippy; rafting up with other canoes is much more stable.

When the wind and weather combine to make traveling impossible or unsafe, you are "wind-bound" or "storm-

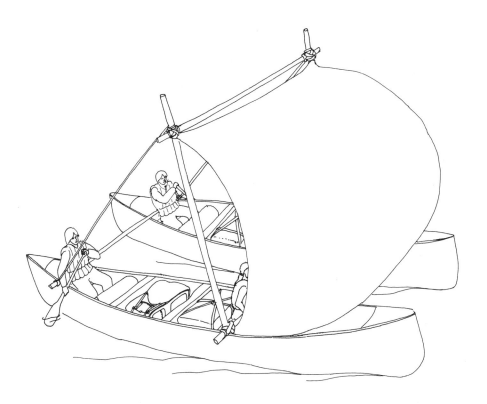

6-3. Catamaran sailing canoe.

bound." Accept that these forces are truly beyond your control and make the most of your day off: bake bannock, eat blueberries, take a nap, read a book, or write in your journal.

LIGHTNING

Lightning is a powerful force, carrying a current of up to fifty million volts and reaching temperatures of fifty thousand degrees Fahrenheit. Every year in the United States lightning is responsible for over one thousand injuries and two hundred to three hundred deaths. Seventy to eighty percent of the people struck by lightning survive. To reduce your chances of getting injured by lightning, learn what to do so you will not find yourself on the water during a thunderstorm.

Watch the sky for signs of a developing thunderstorm: large, dark cumulus clouds building; the distant sounds of rumbling thunder; a brisk breeze increasing; and distant flashes of lightning. Note from which direction the storm is coming and how fast the storm is moving. Sometimes you can see a sheet of rain moving swiftly across an open lake. You can also determine how far away the storm is by counting the seconds between the lightning flash and the clap of thunder. When you see a flash, start counting "one-one-thousand, two-one-thousand, three-one-thousand, four-one-thousand," until you hear the thunder. Take the number of seconds you counted and divide by five; if the lightning flash and thunderclap were five seconds apart, the storm is one mile away. After a few minutes, count again to determine how fast the storm is moving.

When you first see lightning or hear thunder, you should think seriously of getting off the water. Get off the water when the storm is ten miles away or less. Lightning is attracted to water and to the highest object in the water, which is *you!* Water also conducts an electrical charge. If you notice your hair standing up due to static electricity, get off the water fast. This phenomenon, although not always present, indicates the mounting difference of energy between ground and clouds.

Once off the water, seek a place which has minimum chances of attracting lightning. The best shelter is in a clump of trees that are shorter than the surrounding trees. Tall trees are dangerous, as they act as lightning rods. When a tree is struck by lightning, the electricity runs down the trunk and out through the roots. You can insulate yourself from possible ground currents by sitting on your PFD. If you are caught in an open field, lie down to avoid acting as a lightning rod. Groups should spread out to avoid multiple victims injured by ground and side flash currents.

If a friend is knocked unconscious by lightning, first check respiration. If he or she is not breathing, open the airway and start artificial respiration. Check for pulse. If there is no pulse and you are trained, start CPR. Look for other injuries, as a victim can be thrown a considerable distance from the strike site.

Wind, waves, and lightning are powerful forces without regard for paddlers' abilities or schedules. Beware!

7

INTRODUCTION
TO WHITEWATER

AS YOUR FLATWATER PADDLING SKILLS improve, you may
want to paddle whitewater. Before venturing down rapids,
you must learn a few skills so your experience can be a
safe and enjoyable one. This chapter is divided into three
sections: reading whitewater, river maneuvers, and whitewater rescues. We are providing a brief and basic overview
of whitewater paddling. If you are seriously interested in
further developing your whitewater skills, we recommend

you read more detailed books and attend a whitewater school.

READING WHITEWATER

The combination of fast water, rocks, and waves creates patterns in rapids which can indicate, to an experienced whitewater paddler, a clear and safe path through. It is important to recognize basic river patterns in order to understand and respect the forces of moving water. The key to paddling whitewater is to let these forces work for you, not against you.

Currents

Generally, where a river is deep and wide, the current will be slow. Where the same river is shallow and narrow, the current will run faster in order to pass the same volume of water. A drop in the river bed will also create current in a river: a steep drop causes a waterfall while a gentle and gradual drop creates rapids. The current is not constant throughout the river. Water flows faster on the surface and in midstream, since friction slows the water velocity along the bottom and the shores.

In most instances, the current flows parallel to the river banks. The exception to the rule is found in bends, where the strongest current is pushed to the outside of the bend. The current piles up on the outside shore and erodes the bank, often causing trees to fall into the river. These are called *sweepers.* Inexperienced canoeists may find themselves quickly swept to the outside of the bend by these currents.

Eddies are at the very heart of whitewater paddling. They are used as resting places to catch your breath, wait for your friends, or scout the next section of a rapid. Eddies are caused by fast water deflecting around an obstacle. The area behind the obstacle is filled with calm water. When the current is very strong, the water in the eddy will be flowing upstream (fig. 7-1). The place where the river current meets the eddy current is called the *eddy line.*

Rocks

Rocks are easier to locate in fast water because they create wave patterns which indicate their hiding places. When a

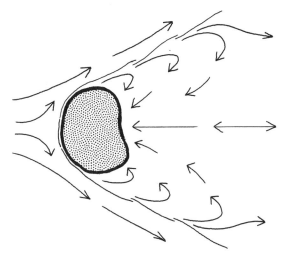

7-1. Current differentials caused by eddy.

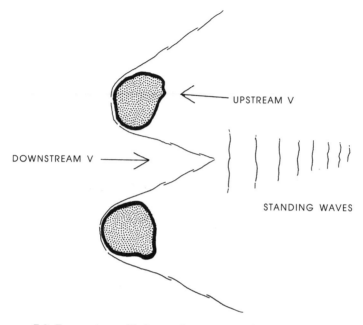

UPSTREAM V

DOWNSTREAM V

STANDING WAVES

7-2. Two upstream V's form a downstream V followed by standing waves.

rock is close to the surface the water flows over it, and a raised, convex wave, called a *pillow,* appears over the rock, with a *following wave* created right behind the rock. As more water flows over the same rock, the following wave appears farther and farther downstream.

A current deflected around rocks will form a V-shaped pattern referred to as an *upstream V.* A *downstream V* is where two upstream Vs meet. This marks a through route (fig. 7-2). A downstream V often has a smooth and glassy appearance and is followed by a set of *standing waves.*

Waves

Standing waves are distinctive, orderly rows of waves which decrease in size and point out a safe route through deeper water. These waves are created when current is constricted into a narrow channel.

A dark horizon line across the river followed by white, foaming waves indicates a powerful current dropping steeply over a ledge. Paddlers refer to this river dynamic as a *hole.* The river current drops to the bottom of the river and rushes along the bottom. The surface water flows upstream to fill the void or hole (fig. 7-3). You can have fun playing in holes found behind rocks but beware of holes caused by ledges and dams. These *keeper holes* (holes strong enough to hold you in) are responsible for many deadly boating incidents.

Scouting

Take the time to study and analyze each set of rapids thor-

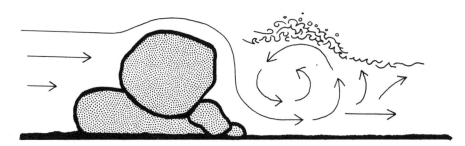

7-3. Water flowing over a drop causes a hole.

oughly. One of the most useful skills of any whitewater canoeist is the ability to look at rapids and decide first if it is runnable and, just as important, whether you and your partner have the skills to run it safely. Not taking the time to "read" a rapid and decide on a route from beginning to end can be a dangerous and foolhardy mistake.

RIVER MANEUVERS

Whitewater canoeing consists of a few basic river maneuvers which use currents to your advantage. Learning and practicing these maneuvers is the best way to ensure that running rapids is safe and fun.

Parallel Side Slip

An easy maneuver to avoid rocks in a slow-moving current is the *side slip.* The bow person picks the route through by moving the front of the canoe to the left or right of the rocks. The stern person quickly moves the back end in the same direction, keeping the canoe parallel to the current (fig. 7-4). The strokes used are the draw and pry. The stern paddler counters with opposite strokes to the bow paddler, for example, a draw in the bow and a pry in the stern. The advantage of the side slip is that it permits you to coast down the rapid at the same speed as the current, allowing you time to scout and pick a route up ahead.

A canoe is not well designed to move sideways; therefore, as the current increases you have less time to move

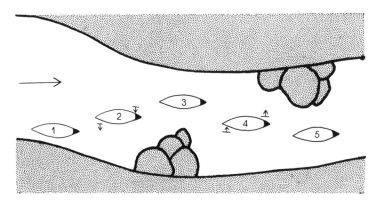

7-4. The slide slip maneuver is used in slow-moving current to avoid rocks.

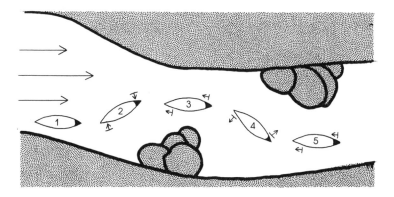

7-5. In fast-moving current, maneuver with forward momentum.

your canoe out of a collision path and must use a different maneuver than the parallel side slip. The bow person, with a quick draw or pry, points the front of the canoe in the desired direction. Both paddlers propel the canoe in the new direction until the middle of the canoe is past the obstacle. The stern person, with a draw or a pry, straightens out the canoe so it is parallel to the current again (fig. 7-5). A canoe moving sideways, even slightly, makes a larger target for a rock, so don't be fooled by the speed of the current and end up broadside on a rock.

Eddy Turns

Eddies often offer superb resting places. To paddle into an eddy you use the *eddy-in* and to leave an eddy the *peel-out.*

To eddy-in, begin by pointing your canoe towards the top of the eddy. Start this maneuver well upstream of the eddy so the current will not carry you past the eddy. Paddle forward and enter the eddy with forward momentum. The moment the bow crosses the eddy line and enters the calm

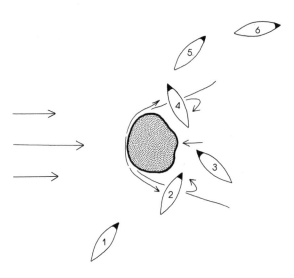

7-6. *Eddy-in:* 1. Drive forward; 2. Cross eddy line at 90° and lean; 3. Pull up into eddy.

   Peel-out: 3. Drive up the eddy; 4. Cross the eddy line at 90° and lean; 5. Hold lean.

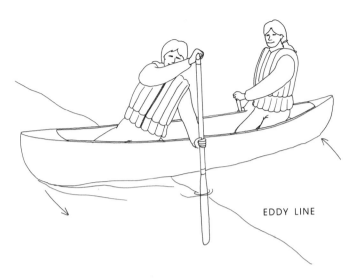

EDDY LINE

7-7. Turning on the eddy line, bow uses a high brace; stern uses a stern forward sweep.

water in the eddy, your canoe will be spun around due to the current differentials. As the canoe spins around you must *lean into the turn* (fig. 7-6, canoes 1, 2, and 3).

Now let's apply strokes to the above maneuver. Suppose you are paddling bow-right and your friend, Eric, is paddling stern-left. You wish to enter into an eddy on the right side of the river. Begin by doing a draw stroke to point the canoe towards the top of the eddy. Paddle forward, and when the front of the canoe crosses the eddy line, you reach out and perform a high brace in the eddy. This stroke allows you to lean the canoe into the turn, similar to leaning a bicycle into a turn. Meanwhile, in the stern, Eric allows you to lean the canoe, and he helps bring the stern into the eddy with a few forward sweep strokes (fig. 7-7). When the canoe has completed its turn, correct your lean and finish with forward strokes to pull the canoe to the top of the eddy.

Let's try the same eddy turn with you paddling bow-left and Eric stern-right. Steer for the top of the eddy, paddle forward, and as the bow crosses the eddy line, you either do a stationary pry or cross draw. Eric helps turn the stern with a reverse sweep and a low brace to lean the canoe into the turn (fig. 7-8).

Here are a few pointers to perfect eddy turns:

1. When approaching an eddy, aim upstream of the eddy to compensate for the speed of the current.

2. The eddy line is strongest at the top of the eddy so enter as close as possible to the top.

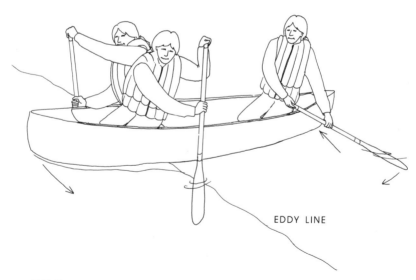

EDDY LINE

7-8. Turning on the eddy line, bow uses pry or cross draw; stern uses a low brace on a reverse sweep.

3. Lean the canoe into the turn. Hold the lean for a few seconds after the turn.

4. Angle of entry

The peel-out is a similar maneuver to the eddy-in, using the same techniques of turning on the eddy line (fig. 7-6, canoes 3, 4, 5, and 6). Paddle forward up the eddy, point the canoe out so it will cross the eddy line at a ninety-degree angle, and lean into the turn. Apply the same combination of strokes as you did entering into eddies (figs. 7-7 and 7-8). It is important to have enough forward speed to carry you out into the current and across the unstable eddy line.

The Forward and Back Ferry

The forward and back ferry are used to get you from one side of the river to the other with the least amount of downstream slip.

In the *forward ferry*, point your canoe upstream and, with forward strokes, paddle against the current. To ferry across the river, set your canoe at about a thirty-degree angle to the current with the bow pointing towards the shore you wish to travel to. The stern person is responsible for setting and maintaining the proper angle to the current (fig. 7-9).

When you set a thirty-degree angle to the current and paddle forward, the forces applied against your canoe move you across the river. Varying your paddling force and/or the angle to the current will determine your final

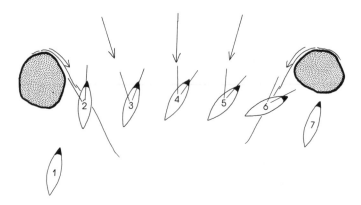

7-9. Forward ferry across current.

direction of travel. The current force against the side of your canoe will also have a tendency to flip your canoe upstream. To counteract this force you must *lean* the canoe downstream. The stronger the current, the more you must lean the canoe.

Moving through current differentials as you forward ferry from one eddy to another can be tricky. Come out of the eddy with enough forward momentum to carry you through the eddy line and into the current. Set a small angle (less than thirty degrees) to the current at the beginning and increase your angle as needed. If you are having problems with the current swinging your bow downstream (peel-out), you will need to cross the eddy line with less angle to the current. Hold your downstream lean and adjust your angle to the main river current. As you approach the other eddy, increase your angle (to more than thirty degrees) to break across the eddy line. Don't forget to reverse your lean and *lean into your turn.*

In theory the *back ferry* is the same as the forward ferry except the canoe is pointing downstream and you are paddling backwards. The angle is set and maintained by the bow paddler. Back ferries can assist you when running rivers. For example, imagine yourself paddling down exciting rapids when you notice the river ahead is impassable except for a small shoot on the far right. You and your partner immediately begin back paddling. The bow paddler sets a thirty-degree angle to the current with the stern pointing to the right-hand shore (fig. 7-10a). Keeping this angle while back paddling will make the canoe glide across the river. Once you are lined up for the shoot, correct your angle and down you go.

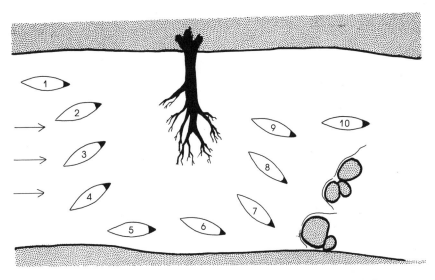

7-10A. Back ferry

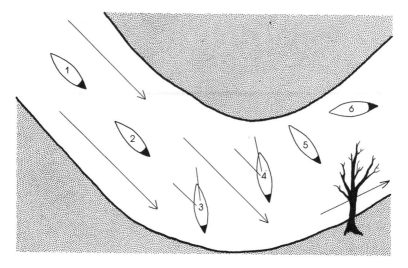

7-10B. Canoes 3 and 4 appear broadside but have a proper back ferry angle to the current. Your angle is relative to the current and not the river bank.

WHITEWATER RESCUES

Whitewater sports have inherent risks. Therefore, it is crucial that you learn and practice basic whitewater rescue skills to minimize or eliminate risk to yourself and others in your party.

Getting Off Rocks

The potential for serious trouble arises when canoes and rocks meet in moving water. You must act quickly and appropriately. As soon as your canoe hits a rock, the current will try to turn the canoe broadside to the current. Once the canoe is broadside to the current, water will pile up on the upstream side and eventually pour in and fill the canoe. You now have a pinned canoe.

Imagine yourself broadside against a large boulder. Quickly lean the canoe downstream to prevent water from pouring in. If the water is shallow, the stern person can get out *upstream* of the canoe and move the canoe off the rock. If the water is fast and deep, the stern person can try to get onto the rock and dislodge the canoe. It is the bow person's responsibility to maintain a downstream lean. Once the canoe is off the rock, guide it into the eddy behind the rock and get back in.

Rescuing Yourself

Sooner or later you will swim in whitewater. The moment you find yourself in whitewater, get to *the upstream side of your canoe!* Move hand over hand along the gunwale or scramble right over the top of the canoe, but get there as

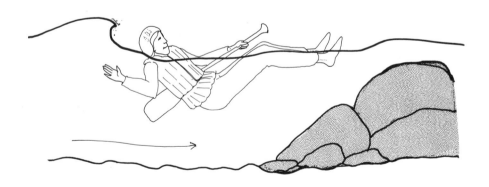

7-11. Swimming a rapid with feet up.

fast as possible. Otherwise you could find yourself pinned and crushed between your canoe and a rock. A capsized seventeen-foot canoe full of water in a six-mile-an-hour current will exert a 3,225-pound force when pinned on an obstacle. *Always* swim upstream of your capsized canoe.

Once you are upstream of your canoe, float on your back with your feet downstream and on the surface of the water (fig. 7-11). It is critical that you keep your feet on the surface to prevent them from becoming wedged between rocks—called a foot entrapment. A foot entrapment can result in death because the water's force on your body will hold you completely submerged. *Never attempt to stand up in moving water that is over knee-deep!* You can stand in very shallow water.

After you are upstream of the canoe and swimming on your back with your feet up, look around for your partner to make sure he or she is okay. Next, pull the painter free and try to keep your canoe parallel to the current. In this position it is less likely to get pinned on a rock. Try to swim and tow the canoe towards shore or an eddy. In most cases your canoe will have a better chance of survival if you stay with it. However, if the water is bitterly cold or the canoe is dangerously out of control, let go and get yourself to shore as quickly as possible. Make sure you stay on your back with your feet downstream and on the surface.

Rescuing Others

The best way to rescue paddlers floating in whitewater is to use a *throw line rescue bag.* They are available at most whitewater stores. To throw, open the top of the bag, grab the end of the rope in your left hand, and throw the bag underarm. The weight of the bag will carry the rope straight out. Your aim is very important. If your target is moving in the current, you must aim slightly downstream. If your friend is stranded on a rock, aim upstream, and the current will carry the rope to him or her. When the swimmer grabs the rope, sit down and brace yourself for a tug as the line becomes taut, and the swimmer swings into shore.

Rescuing Canoes

Once your friends are safe, you must turn your attention to rescuing the canoe. Canoes are easiest to rescue in the calm pools below rapids, where you can push or tow the canoe to shore or perform a canoe over canoe rescue. It is important to perform the rescue before the canoe and possibly yourself get sucked down the next rapid.

If a canoe becomes pinned on a rock, take the time to formulate a good and safe plan of action. Don't put yourself and your friends at greater risk by attempting a hasty rescue. In shallow water, a few people may be able to lift the upstream gunwale and pull the canoe off the rock. Getting people out to the canoe may require setting up a safety line to use as a handrail.

If the water is too fast and deep to get people out to the canoe, you must use ropes to pull the canoe from shore. Ferry out to the eddy behind the pinned canoe. Tie your throw line rope *around* the end of the canoe (a strong pull will rip off the painter ring or deck). If your party is large enough, you might be able to free the canoe. If not, you must use a mechanical advantage system such as a Z drag with climbing pulleys and carabiners or a lightweight come-along.

Sweepers

Sweepers are trees which have fallen across the river and are blocking part or all of the river. A sweeper allows the current to pass through but larger objects like canoes or swimmers can get trapped in the submerged branches.

When you encounter a sweeper:

1. Recognize it as dangerous.

2. Stay clear of it. Since they are most often found at bends in the river, be aware of the direction of the current and set your ferry angle accordingly.

3. If you find yourself heading into a sweeper, try to climb up onto it to prevent getting sucked down by the current.

Paddling whitewater is exhilarating: the rush of fast-moving water, the big splash as you plunge through the standing waves, or the feeling of accomplishment as you pull into the last eddy at the bottom of a challenging rapid. Good judgment on your part will ensure a *safe* and enjoyable whitewater experience. Good judgment comes from the ability to read whitewater and assess if you have the skills to run the rapid, practiced river maneuvers, and a keen eye and quick mind to execute the proper rescue when needed.

8

ENVIRONMENT

As our wilderness areas become fewer and more crowded, our definition of pollution and our wilderness ethics must change. What respected wilderness travelers did in the past is sometimes considered poor practice today. Once it was considered proper trail ethics to crush, burn, and bury cans; to sleep on a mattress of green pine boughs; or to cut and lash log-pole lean-tos and tables. Today these practices are frowned upon.

Not only do the rules keep changing as our world becomes more polluted, but environmental practices that are acceptable in one area are destructive in another environment. For example, in parts of northern Ontario there is an abundant supply of firewood, but high in the Rocky Mountains firewood is scarce.

This chapter will increase your awareness of the problems your impact on wilderness areas can create and encourage you to move through the wilderness leaving as little trace as possible. This chapter will examine: what is considered garbage and how to deal with it; drinking water; the use of fires versus stoves; and the evolution of park rules to deal with the growing problems of human impact.

GARBAGE

Twenty years ago it was acceptable to leave decomposable garbage in the wilderness. By this standard tin cans, pine bough mattresses, and lashed log tables were all considered decomposable. Today it is unacceptable to leave any sign the next wilderness traveler will see. In very remote wilderness areas it could be years before the next traveler comes along; in more populated areas it could be ten minutes. You must also determine what will and will not decompose in various environments. Most organic waste will decompose faster in warm, wet environments than in dry, desert environments.

Human waste, such as feces and urine, is a complex

problem. In the Grand Canyon National Park, rafters and boaters on the Colorado River are required to pack out all garbage, including their feces and toilet paper in portable potties. Even dishwater must be strained and the little bits of food and goop packed out. The park requires visitors to urinate in the river because the smell of urine in the sand is very strong. Grand Canyon National Park is an example of a heavily used, fragile environment where decomposition is very slow. At the other extreme, in warm, wet environments, feces decompose quickly when buried. In northern Ontario it is common practice to bury feces a few inches under the soil. Bacteria-laden human feces must be buried well away from water sources. Toilet paper must always be carried out or burned.

Cans must be burned, crushed, and carried out. Burning the cans eliminates smells which may attract animals to your campsite.

Glass should not be carried on the trail since it is heavy and breakable. You can purchase plastic food bottles at camping stores for jam, peanut butter, and margarine, or reuse the plastic containers in which some foods are packaged.

Plastic is a nonrenewable resource and is considered nonbiodegradable. Carry out all plastic products, since burning them causes air pollution. Often campfires aren't hot enough to burn the plastic, and the plastic simply melts.

Paper should be burned in your campfire or carried out.

Leftover food presents a problem. If you bury it, animals will smell it, dig it up, and scatter it all over. Too often bits and globs of oatmeal and noodles are left in the water at well-used campsites. Unfortunately, the fish will not eat it. Small amounts of leftover food should be burned in your campfire or carried out. The best solution is to bring just the right amount of food, cook it with care, and eat it all.

Soap There are many biodegradable soaps on the market. *But* washing in rivers and lakes does not improve drinking water and is therefore inappropriate. Don't do it! One way to wash and not pollute the lake or river is to soap up away from the water and rinse off with a few pots full of water before taking the final plunge. Forgo the use of scented soaps, as they attract mosquitoes and black flies. After washing cups, bowls, and pots, heave the dishwashing soap far into the woods.

WATER

"Water, water, everywhere, but not a drop to drink." North America was once blessed with an endless supply of drinking water. Now much of it is contaminated with industrial pollutants, acid rain, chemical fertilizers, giardia, and human feces. Today the question "to drink or not to drink" is part of our wilderness vocabulary. There are three common methods of water purification: boiling your water, adding iodine, or using a portable trail filter.

Boiling your cooking and drinking water is a safe method of killing off bacteria and germs provided you boil the water four minutes or longer. To boil all your water is time-consuming and often inconvenient. If you are using stoves it will mean carrying more fuel.

Iodizing your water is another option. Iodine can be obtained in tablet, crystal, or eyedropper form. The amount of iodine needed to kill bacteria and germs depends on the temperature of the water and the length of time the iodine is in the water. Make sure you follow the directions supplied with the iodine. Note that the use of iodine is not recommended for pregnant women, for people with thyroid problems, or for an extended period of time.

The safest water purification system is a *good* filter which will filter out giardia cysts and other unwanted critters. Pumping through a filter is slow. In areas where all your water must be treated, consider carrying a pump for every four persons.

FIRES VERSUS STOVES

In the Arctic, desert areas, alpine mountaintops, or New York City, it is necessary to carry a stove (or carry food which does not require cooking). In forested areas the question you should consider is, "Am I having a more negative impact on the environment by using a fire or by using a cook stove?" Although stoves leave no fire scars, when you consider the big picture you realize a stove uses highly refined oil. This product is a nonrenewable resource which, through extracting, processing, and transporting, is responsible for a great deal of pollution. In areas of abundant dead, downed wood, use a fire. In high-use areas use a stove.

Collecting firewood can leave longlasting signs. Avoid cutting green wood (live trees) and *never strip bark off a live tree.* Look for dead wood on the forest floor. Along a beach you can collect driftwood. Break off the branches to avoid the obvious sawed-off-branch look. During rainy periods, you can find dry wood among the bottom branches of coniferous trees.

If a fire pit exists at a campsite, *use it.* Do not build another fire pit a few feet away from an already existing one. Even in very remote areas, you can still build a fire and not leave permanent scars. The three common methods are:

1. Whenever possible, build your fire on the sand. When you are done, burn all the wood down to ashes. Make certain your fire is out, then scatter the ashes and darkened sand on the forest floor.

2. If there is no sand available, find a flat rock or rocks upon which you can build your fire. When you are done, burn all the wood down to ashes, put your fire out, and throw the ashes and rocks into the forest, lake, or river.

3. The last option is to gently pull away the topsoil and stack it under a nearby tree. Build your fire on the ground. When you are done, burn the wood down to ashes, put the fire out, scatter the ashes, and place the topsoil back where it belongs.

PARK RULES AND REGULATIONS

If you are planning a canoe trip in a national, state, or provincial park, write ahead for park rules and regulations. Parks may have restrictions on the use of campfires, bans on cans and bottles, limitations on group size, or requirements concerning the use of designated campsites. Some heavily used parks require campsite reservations and restrict the number of people in the park.

WILDERNESS RESPONSIBILITIES

We need and want clean, unpolluted open spaces where we can relax, reflect, and adventure. What are we willing to give up in order to get what we want? Will rules, regulations, and fines protect our wilderness areas, or must we do more?

If we truly care for our natural environment, we *must* become more responsible. This happens when you and I take responsibility for our own actions *and* do more than our share. It makes a strong statement to carry out more garbage than you brought in or to take fifteen minutes to write a letter to your government representative requesting more parks and wild rivers. It all starts with us and our individual actions at home and in the wilderness. There is no excuse for leaving traces of our passage in the wilderness. It is now an obligation for wilderness travelers to leave the area traveled through cleaner than when they arrived.

INDEX